9.17.79

The Joy of
EXPENSE
ACCOUNT
LIVING

& the Pleasures of Executive Perks

SIDNEY RUTBERG

Contemporary Books, Inc.
Chicago

Library of Congress Cataloging in Publication Data

Rutberg, Sidney.
    The joy of expense account living.

    Includes index.
    1. Expense accounts—United States.   I. Title.
HD4965.3.R87 1979   331.2'55   79-50990
ISBN 0-8092-7400-0

Published by Contemporary Books, Inc.
180 North Michigan Avenue, Chicago, Illinois 60601
Manufactured in the United States of America
Library of Congress Catalog Card Number: 79-50990
International Standard Book Number: 0-8092-7400-0

Published simultaneously in Canada by
Beaverbooks
953 Dillingham Road
Pickering, Ontario L1W 1Z7
Canada

To my wife, Adele,
who is a joy with or
without an expense account

Contents

"When President Carter suggested that the three-martini business lunch be abolished as a tax deduction, a wave of terror swept over the expense account set. . . . However, it soon became clear that the chances of eliminating the expense account lunch were about as large as the smile on the face of a waiter who has just been stiffed by a party of eight."

Sidney Rutberg—a veteran of the "expense account wars"—should be the mentor of everyone who has an expense account, the inspiration of everyone who wants an expense account, and the favorite story-teller of everyone who dreams of the audacious luxury-living of expense account high-rollers. He tells us unabashedly, "The knowledge that two tickets to a hit musical or dinner at '21' will have no impact on your own financial condition is one of the greatest pleasures of twentieth-century civilization." He confirms our suspicion that, in the expense account world, sex is a form of tax-deductible entertainment. And he helps the reader unravel the tangle of government and business over the taxability of perquisites—fringe benefits that enable corporate superstars to maintain their fabulous life-styles.

The Joy of Expense Account Living counsels women who have expense accounts to abandon the housewifely ethos of frugality; it encourages them to join in the money power-play of business relationships. It offers the business-luncher

If you are fascinated by the life-styles of the wealthy, *The Joy of Expense Account Living* will provide you with case histories that reveal how the big expense account manipulators *really* live, and how they obtain their wealth. It will leave you gaping. And it may leave you wondering—about the possibilities for the expense account in your own future.

Introduction to Expense Account Living

WHEN PRESIDENT CARTER SUGGESTED that the three-martini business lunch be abolished as a tax deduction, a wave of terror swept over the expense account set. Although three martinis had long ago been largely replaced by Perrier water and lime or a glass of white wine, a great American principle was at stake: *There is no such thing as a free lunch, but the expense account meal comes pretty damned close.*

Those enjoying the authority to sign for a forty dollar lunch-for-two at Michael's Pub or the Italian Pavilion were panicked. However, calmer heads prevailed, and it soon became clear that the chances of eliminating the expense account lunch were about as large as the smile on the face of a waiter who has just been stiffed by a party of eight.

Representative Al Ullman, Chairman of the House Ways and Means Committee—the congressional unit that initiates all tax legislation—soon spoke out firmly against tampering with this great tradition. Representative Ullman expressed the fear that hotels and restaurants would be devastated if the President's suggestion ever were to become law. Said Ullman: "We're not going to pass a tax bill that puts half of America out of business."

While Ullman may have been indulging in a bit of hyperbole, there is no doubt that the expense account is so deeply enmeshed in the workings of our economy that serious dislocations would result even if only half the cost of a business meal were not deductible. As a veteran of the expense account circuit, I would be extremely reluctant to pick up a thirty dollar check for a business lunch if I had to pay fifteen dollars of it out of my own pocket. I would more likely spend three bucks at the local coffee shop and the rest of my lunch hour browsing through book shops.

What finally emerged in the Revenue Act of 1978, passed in the closing hours of the Ninety-fifth Congress and signed with little enthusiasm by President Carter, was a masterpiece of tokenism. Barred as deductions were the costs of "facilities" used for business entertainment, such as yachts, hunting lodges, fishing camps, swimming pools, tennis courts, and bowling alleys. However, "country club" dues were specifically exempted from the statute, and could still be deducted as business expenses. The language of the statute led to a flap over the question of whether the dues of "clubs" other than country clubs would qualify as deductions. (See chapter ten, "The Revenue Act of 1978.")

As is the case with any law, the Revenue Act of 1978 is subject to various interpretations by the courts and administrative agencies; so there is no assurance that the opinions of accountants or of any other tax experts will stand up. But there appears to be little danger that the Revenue Act will put much of a dent in expense account living. Talk about business overspending on entertainment will continue, and politicians will rail about the injustice of it all. But fear not, the expense account will not become extinct. At the moment, it's not even an endangered species.

Aside from the fact that so many American businesses

survive solely on the travel, entertainment, and promotional expenditures of other businesses, the people who make and/or administer our laws are no strangers to expense account living, and many have perks that equal or surpass those of top executives in the private sector.

If we accept the expense account as a continuing fact of business life, men and women should learn to deal with it and profit from it. I think women have special problems in adjusting to the free-spending ways of business. The feminist movement has impelled an ever-increasing number of women into the labor force (inflation has also had a hand in swelling the ranks of working women), and as time goes on more and more will be in positions which provide expense accounts and perks.

As relative newcomers to the great American expense account subculture, women are particularly in need of guidance. They must cope with the leftovers of male chivalry (or chauvinism) and also must deal with their own inexperience. Women conditioned as housewives or mothers have worked with limited budgets and are prone to skimp rather than spend lavishly. That tendency must be overcome if they are to take their rightful places in the expense account society.

Women who never have been exposed to conditioning as housewives—those who were career oriented from childhood—still must operate, at check-paying time, in an environment in which women are seen as entertainees rather than as entertainors. Eventually, our culture will come to accept the sight of a woman paying a check for a man. But, at the moment, male pride and society's perception of the male and female roles remain realities to be dealt with.

Once mastered, expense account living provides you with a peace of mind that can never be achieved while spending your own money. The guilt that goes with self-indulgence at the expense of other members of your family is virtually eliminated, since expense account money is not transferable. The knowledge that an extravagant lunch or two tickets to a hit musical or dinner at 21 Club ('21') will have no impact on your own financial condition is one of the greatest pleasures of twentieth-century civilization. Others wait fearfully for the monthly batch of bills to arrive, but with an expense account you just spend it and forget it.

Russell Baker, my favorite *New York Times* columnist, in a piece on the culture within a commercial airliner, points out how sharp are the contrasts between the privileged expense account traveler and the run-of-the-plane tourist. Baker observes:

> Behind the pilot sit the first-class passengers in comfortable seats. Most commonly, they seem to be businessmen traveling on expense accounts.
>
> These men are concerned with establishing their positions in the hierarchical order, which they do by asking each other, "Who are you with?" To be with one of *Fortune*'s 500 biggest corporations is superior to being with yourself. Being with the federal government is better than being with the government of Biloxi, Miss. And so on. It is very rare for anyone to ask, "What are you interested in?" or "What does it all mean?" Gathering information of this sort is not considered commercially justifiable on an expense account.
>
> Behind the first-class section sit the people who, for the most part, have paid for their own tickets. Their seats are cramped and jammed uncomfortably close together. This is consistent with the national policy that people who do not enjoy tax deductibility must be made to suffer.

And suffer you will, unless you join in the fun. The way to go is to seek out the areas where you can live in tax deductible comfort on expense accounts and executive perquisites (perks). This book will help identify areas where expense accounts are to be found, show how to get there, how to use your expense account to its maximum potential, where to find those golden perks, and how sweet they are.

While the garden variety expense account can provide free meals, free entertainment, and free travel, with perks you can enter a world of Park Avenue apartments, chauffeured limousines, country club memberships . . . in short, all the accoutrements of the good life.

The joys of expense account living and executive perks go beyond the activities spelled out in expense reports and corporate prospectuses. You won't find "it" listed in any of the handbooks on executive compensation, either. "It" is S-E-X. Just how much tax deductible corporate cash goes for supplying the pleasures of the flesh would be impossible to calculate, and any estimate would constitute the rawest of speculation. However, in a competitive environment, where prices and quality are often similar throughout the market, the seller needs some kind of an edge to get preference over a rival. Sex could be that edge.

Any discussion of expense accounts and perks must deal with the Internal Revenue Service, the folks who make it all possible. The IRS is charged with monitoring the reasonableness of travel and entertainment (T&E) deductions, and with answering such questions as whether some real corporate purpose is served when the boss takes his blond secretary with him on a business trip to Atlantic City. The IRS can be tough under some circumstances and the soul of sweet reason at other times. In this book, we will look inside the IRS and tell you what you can probably get away with and what is likely to bring the tax man down on your head.

There are two ways to beat the tax man—evasion or avoidance. Evasion is an illegal method of avoiding taxes. Avoidance is a legal method of evading taxes. This book will endeavor to define the blurred line between the two and show how the expense account can serve to avoid, but not evade, taxes.

Before the revenue people ever get a crack at you, you will encounter a level of expense account supervision much closer to home—your company's own accounting department. It is not the purpose of this volume to explain how to rip off your company, but rather to show how you can legitimately extract the greatest benefits for yourself.

At this point, I should offer a few words of caution. The

human tendency to overdo a good thing is present in all of us. In my search for spectacular examples of luxury living on other people's money, I have stumbled on some truly awesome cases—some that fall in the gray area between self-indulgence and larceny and others that are clearly criminal. Details of these corporate delights became available because some government agency or other learned that someone was taking too much too soon. In other words, he got caught. (The masculine pronoun will be used throughout this book to avoid the awkward use of he/she.) So, before going ahead, I'd like to say that lots of room is out there in the expense account club for new members and mountains of money are there to be spent. Enjoy, but don't get greedy. Nothing can snuff out the charm of expense account living more completely than getting caught abusing a system that asks so little and offers so much to those who simply play by the rules.

CHAPTER ONE

The Good Life

Maximizing Profits with the Least Pain

THE RESTAURANT was in New York City's fashionable East Sixties. Thirty guests—the women elegantly gowned and jeweled, the men impeccably attired—sipped cocktails and made small talk for ninety minutes. Then everyone sat down to a dinner of smoked scotch salmon, *foie gras en bloc,* truffle soup, roast veal (from calves fed only milk for fifty-odd days of their lives), baked apple slices, glazed carrots, and sautéed green beans. This rich fare was washed down with champagne, fourteen bottles of red and white wine and three bottles of port (vintage, 1937, $150 a bottle).

Music was provided by a trio, and, with the service of the truffle soup, the party came alive with community singing and dancing. At the end of the evening, the group sang "Auld Lang Syne," after which the happy troop retired to waiting, chauffeured limos.

The bill for this entertainment—$6,000. The cost to the guests—zero. It was a dinner given by the Sperry Rand

Corporation for its board of directors and members of its international advisory board. The $6,000 was paid out of corporate funds and deducted from taxable income as part of the expense of doing business. The dinner was much like thousands of others run by business organizations, the only difference being that a reporter from the *Wall Street Journal* was present at this one.

The affair was held at the posh Le Premier Restaurant on East 63rd Street. Guests, according to the *Wall Street Journal* account, included the chairman of the investment banking firm of Blyth Eastman Dillon; the chairman of textile giant J. P. Stevens and Company; a former Secretary of State; the president of the Metropolitan Life Insurance Company; an international shipping magnate; and, of course, Sperry Rand's top brass. Wives were invited.

The business portion of the dinner was a brief speech by J. Paul Lyet, chairman of Sperry Rand, about how well the company was doing and, according to the *Journal*, "a few minutes of jokes." Although business was "touched on" in the social setting, most of the talk, the *Journal* observed, was "typical cocktail party chitchat."

Would the cost of this affair be treated as a business expense? You bet. Sperry Rand chairman, Lyet, told the *Journal*, "This board is very helpful to us. Having a social evening right before the business meeting permits us to discuss some things we can't do at the meeting." (The dinners are held semiannually, the night before a scheduled business meeting.)

Whether a $200-a-plate dinner constitutes a waste of corporate funds or really helps to "maximize profits" is not the point here. The point is, expense account living can be a real blast. The IRS merely requires that a "substantial" business discussion take place just prior to, during, or immediately following the entertainment. There is yet to be a directive to the effect that if business entertainment is fun, it's not deductible.

Opportunities to participate in fun and games while attending business meetings are widely advertised: "People are often amazed to learn that some of the most luxurious resorts in the country host business meetings." This headline kicked off a mouthwatering advertising section that ran in a number of slick business publications (*Forbes,* October 2, 1978, among others) describing the facilities and recreational activities available for sales meetings, conventions, and other business get-togethers. The section was lavishly illustrated, in full color, with photographs of golf courses, lakes, boats, magnificent buildings, and even an occasional meeting room.

I was not amazed, having regularly covered an annual convention at the posh Boca Raton Hotel and Club in Boca Raton, Florida, one of the resorts included in the ad (rates, modified American plan, $95 to $165 a day, single; $110 to $180, double). The hotel in Boca features four eighteen-hole golf courses, twenty tennis courts, three swimming pools, a cabana club on the ocean, a health club, deep-sea fishing, and more. In short, the Boca Raton Hotel and Club virtually guarantees that any business meeting held there will not get bogged down in a lot of business. (The group I have covered schedules meetings for the morning, leaving afternoons free for tennis, golf, swimming, and sunning; and the evenings free for dining, dancing, drinking, and fooling around.)

The advertisement which ran in *Forbes* justified resort meetings as "a great way to motivate your people." The pitch continued, "There's nothing like holding your meeting at a well-known resort to put people in a positive frame of mind for doing business. The prestige, the ambiance, the incomparable amenities, the natural beauty of the surroundings . . . those are the things that make for great involvement and enthusiasm at a meeting." You can bet your ass that there will be enthusiasm and involvement. But business? I don't know.

The thirty-two resorts represented in the *Forbes* ad section were broken down by location. Among those representing the Midwest/East were the Concord Hotel at Kiamesha Lake, New York—with forty-five holes of golf and twenty-eight indoor and outdoor tennis courts—and its Catskill Mountain neighbor, Grossinger's—with a mere twenty-seven holes of golf and sixteen tennis courts. The Montauk Yacht Club and Inn, Star Island, out on the tip of Long Island, could only offer golf and tennis "nearby" but made up for these shortcomings by providing, "excellent deep-sea fishing, bicycling, sailing, water sports, and a spa complete with a Jacuzzi, sauna, exercise rooms, and an indoor pool. The dining is superb, and five elegant rooms are available for relaxed meetings in tranquil surroundings."

In the Midwest, there is Boyne Country, which includes Boyne Mountain and Boyne Highlands in Northern Michigan—a resort complex which boasts seventy-two holes of championship golf, skiing, sailing, swimming, and fishing. All this is available, the ad says, "without your ever leaving either of the resorts."

Another famous, old, rest and recreation spot that is pushing for business meetings is the Greenbrier of White Sulphur Springs, West Virginia, a plantationlike layout operated as though the Civil War never was fought. "They don't really employ slaves," one recent visitor told me, "but they do their best to keep their guests from finding that out." The Greenbrier also has lots of golf (fifty-four holes including eighteen designed by Jack Nicklaus) and all the rest, from horseback riding to bowling.

Moving farther South we have the Pinehurst Hotel and Country Club, Pinehurst, North Carolina, "Site of the World Golf Hall of Fame" and "the only resort in America with six championship courses."

I might mention at this point that the ad section featured Jack Nicklaus, who was quoted as saying that "resorts are a great place to do business." Judging from the emphasis of the ad copy, his statement is supremely accurate—if you're in the same business as Nicklaus.

Representing the West, we have the Hotel del Coronado, near San Diego, where the weather is "perfect" year-round, and the executive, "in a superb garden setting," can feel he's "truly earned a sumptuous meal in one of the exquisite dining salons" after a day of tennis, golf, or swimming.

Another standout in the West is The Lodge, at Pebble Beach in California. For eighty to ninety dollars a day (without food), the executive can attend a business meeting at the home of "the world-renowned Bing Crosby Golf Tournament" and can find "excellent accommodations, superb cuisine, an extensive wine cellar, and outstanding facilities to create the ideal environment for meetings and relaxation."

There are, of course, many other plush resorts catering to business meetings, but there is no point in mentioning additional ones. It should be clear by now that an awful lot of good living is going on, and to get in on the enjoyment, nothing can substitute for the old expense account. You may have to listen to a few dreary speeches, or miss a putt or two to avoid humiliating your boss, but the price is right.

Expense account living can be found in the most unlikely places. Take the New York subway system—grimy, smelly, graffiti-ridden—the last place one might expect to find a life of luxury. Yet top officials of the Metropolitan Transportation Authority (MTA) and the Transit Authority (TA), the quasi-public agency that runs the system, seem to live nicely with expense account help.

Unfortunately, the MTA (the umbrella agency for the Long Island Railroad and other transit facilities in the New York Metropolitan area) and the TA (which operates the New York City subway and bus systems) consistently pile up massive deficits which must be covered by tax revenues. Thus, lavish living in these agencies will generate more than a passing interest among New York City's taxpayers. An investigation by the *New York Daily News* into expense accounts of transit officials turned up a $100,000-a-year round of world-travel, first-class hotels, meals at the city's finest restaurants, and luxury cars with chauffeurs on twenty-four-hour call.

A review of the expense reports of the four top officials showed that they alone spent almost $20,000 on travel and more than $6,000 on lunches and dinners during a fifteen-month period. The *News* reported that the officials ate regularly with their staffs at such restaurants as '21', and the head of the TA billed the agency for fifty-five meals at such eateries as The Club on the 107th floor of the World Trade Center, the Whitehall Club in New York's financial district, and the Old Homestead Steak House. Forty-six of those meals, costing a total of $3,266, were with his own staff to discuss internal matters, such as personnel and budget.

The agency's chief was also much traveled in the period under review, spending about $10,000 on thirteen trips, principally to attend transit conferences. Among the sites: London, England; Stuttgart, Germany; Lyon, France; Boca Raton, Florida; and Monterey, California. (Ten to one the Boca Raton trip was at the Boca Raton Hotel and Club, and the Monterey jaunt at Pebble Beach.)

Within a few days after the *News*'s story—which was headlined, "TA Execs Wine and Dine Oh-So-Fine on Thine"—appeared in print, the TA issued a new set of expense account guidelines. In announcing the new guidelines, the MTA chairman said that they had been drawn up, not because of any impropriety by officials, but because the agency had never had any guidelines. He denied that the *News*'s story had anything to do with new guidelines, but claimed that they had been brought about by the account scandal at the Port Authority (PA) of New York and New Jersey. Details of the free-spending PA will be discussed later. In any event, the new guidelines prohibited use of expense accounts for intramural lunches and tightened up on personal use of automobiles.

Said MTA chief Harold L. Fisher, "It's a question of people knowing what they should or should not do. What they should not do, according to the guidelines, is pay for a meal at which a Transportation Authority staff member is entertained—even if it is a business meeting—and then submit an expense account for reimbursement." In other words, fellas, it's okay to eat at the '21'; just be sure you have someone from outside the agency eating with you.

Since it is now fairly obvious that expense accounts can

provide the good things in life, the next question that must be dealt with is how to justify your expenditures. Is there a good business reason for all this lavish living (the IRS specifically forbids deductions for "lavish" expenses, but there is a problem defining lavish), or is the practice a rip-off of business and the government? The answer is yes. It all depends on your point of view.

Treasury Secretary W. Michael Blumenthal, who left the chairmanship of the Bendix Corporation to join the Carter Administration, charged that some of the lavish entertainment expenses of big business resulted in the average taxpayer's subsidizing "the untaxed personal consumption of some of the most affluent Americans." He made this statement as part of his campaign in support of his boss's program to tighten up the tax laws and eradicate the three-martini lunch. Prior to aligning himself with the Carter camp, Blumenthal, as head of Bendix, had the use of a company-financed box for the Forest Hills Tennis matches and his choice of 200 season tickets to Notre Dame football games. The tickets were held by Bendix to be used for business entertainment.

The justification for travel and entertainment (T&E) expenditures is that they purportedly bring in new business and preserve existing business and, as *Fortune* magazine put it in an article defending expense accounts and executive perks, "maximize profits." There is little doubt that T&E expenditures will make some contribution to the revenues of any corporation. The real issue is the cost-benefit ratio. What do you get for what you spend? Fortunately for those who would enjoy the benefits of expense account living, there is no way to determine accurately whether a dollar spent on T&E will bring in ten dollars in new profits, or fifty cents, or will net out to a loss. However, there is evidence that T&E outlays serve some corporate purpose.

One basis for judging the benefits which accrue to corporations as a result of expense accounts and perks is overall business success. A strong argument for liberal business spending might be made by citing the example of Japan.

Since their country was rebuilt out of the ashes of World War II, the Japanese have been the most aggressive and successful businessmen in the world. They have attained dominance in world markets in one field after another: cameras, color televisions, radios, hi-fi equipment, calculators, mini-computers, digital watches. And Japan has the most pervasive system of perks and expense account living in the world. Executive salaries are quite low by American standards, but Japanese corporations sweeten the pot with country club memberships (which in Japan are incredibly expensive), automobiles, apartments, meals, etc.

The Japanese system, called Kosai-hi, is carefully structured. Top executives might spend $300 a person for an evening's entertainment at an elegant tea house or a private club, with transportation provided by the ubiquitous chauffeured limousine. Lower ranked executives might have to be satisfied with a restaurant meal and an evening of bar-hopping. This might run $150 a head. Minor functionaries have to keep the charge down to $50 for two. (These are all 1978 prices and should be adjusted for inflation).

A New York public relations man told me the following story, which he swears is true. He was on a business trip in Japan, traveling with a Japanese author. In the course of conversation, the Japanese asked if the American had an expense account.

"Sure," the PR man replied.

"So have I," said the Japanese, "Let's go into this store and buy our wives fur coats on expenses."

The American gulped a little and, in order not to lose face, advised his free-spending friend that he had purchased a fur coat for his wife within the past week and didn't want to overdo it. Whereupon the Japanese went into the store, picked out a mink coat for his wife, and charged it to his publisher; while the PR man, who regarded himself as something of a master of the art of creative expenses, stood by in complete awe.

As in the United States, there is a major sector of the

Japanese economy that feeds on Kosai-hi, and tampering with it would cause major economic dislocations. Figures on the cost of Kosai-hi are hard to come by, but an estimate provided to *Fortune* by the National Tax Administration puts the figure at about two percent of Japan's gross national product. This is considerably higher than estimates of such expenditures by United States business, but United States estimates are at best unreliable and at worst completely fictitious. As of this writing, the IRS has no idea how much money is spent on T&E because until 1978, corporate tax forms did not have a line on which T&E was broken out. Now they have, but it will be a couple of years before the IRS gets around to tabulating the figures.

Japan has been successful in business, and the Japanese spend freely on business entertainment, but this doesn't prove that large T&E expenses equal success in business. Spending money on entertainment is not the only factor in Japanese business success. Their work force is fiercely loyal and hard-working; the Japanese are great savers and, thus, supply funds for investment in modern equipment; and the Japanese government is in bed with business—working to promote Japanese corporate interest throughout the world. On the other hand, the fact that the Japanese spend so much on T&E and still manage to be successful does prove that it's possible to piss away a lot of money on entertainment without any apparent damage to the corporate structure.

Although there are no reasonable estimates of expenditures by United States business on T&E, *Fortune,* in the article defending expense accounts and perks, came up with an estimate based on an IRS study done in 1969. The figures were compiled from returns of 16,221 companies with assets of less than $1 million and mathematically projected to take in all of American business. The figures were updated to 1976 by adding an inflation factor based on increases in the cost of goods sold. The number that emerged from this method of mathematical masturbation was $16,395,000,000 in 1976, up from $1,799,000,000 in 1969.

A couple of the more obvious weaknesses in the statistical methodology: The smaller the company the more it will lie about its T&E expenditures, so the selection of companies with less than $1 million in assets is probably the worst sample available; and inflation tends to compound T&E expenses, since rising prices certainly encourage broader expense account use.

The largest component of the Treasury Department figure was travel, which represented seventy-one percent of total T&E both in 1969 and 1976. It is a dubious assumption, indeed, that there has been no change in the mix over that period. Furthermore, the figures focused on T&E and, while this would take in some of the expenditures on executive perks, millions of dollars spent on the care and comforts of top executives would be classified in other categories, such as general administrative expenses or home office expenses.

As long as the United States Treasury was prepared to estimate T&E expenditures on a purely arbitrary basis, why shouldn't I. The nation's gross national product (GNP) is currently running in the neighborhood of two trillion dollars ($2,000,000,000,000). Assuming that T&E expenses here are about two percent of GNP, we're talking about $40 billion.

In its defense of perks and expense account living, the *Fortune* article noted that President Carter's bid to curtail the good business life specifically tackled the question of "enjoyment." Business entertainment "must produce personal enjoyment to have its intended effect" said the president; thus, it represents private enrichment at public expense. Not so, says *Fortune:* "If the money spent on T&E is productive—i.e., if it serves to maximize net income—then no subsidy is involved. Rather, the spending for this purpose will produce larger net profits for government to tax. From an economic standpoint, it would make no more sense to disallow deductions for T&E than to disallow deductions for salaries, capital equipment, or anything else that is supposed to generate profits."

Fortune also cites a much quoted analogy attributed to Senate Finance Committee chairman, Russell Long, that "entertainment is to the selling business what fertilizer is to the farming business."

Fortune found that while there was no question in the minds of businessmen that all this high living was justifiably business related, there was a certain reticence about going into detail. Such defenders of free enterprise as General Motors, General Electric, and Bethlehem Steel refused to discuss the subject. And those that did pointed out that business entertainment is not a simple cause and effect relationship.

Said a DuPont vice-president in talking about the 125 club memberships the company pays for: "We use these clubs to establish the kind of relationship we want to have with our customers or even with our suppliers. It's a long-range process. We don't play golf with Mr. X to pull off some deal. That's a phony concept. We want our customers to feel comfortable with us so, in a close call, the business goes our way."

An executive of another company spoke of using a hunting lodge to create "an atmosphere conducive to understanding." More colorful is the statement by literary agent Irving "Swifty" Lazar, who regularly puts together million-dollar deals for celebrity authors. Says Swifty to *Fortune:* "Jimmy Carter's a hick. He's not going to change the way people do business. Put a guy you're doing a million-dollar deal with in a taxi and he's cold. Put him in a limousine and he's warm. A customer has a sense of elation eating dinner at the 21 Club, a feeling of gaiety going to a play. That's business, my friend."

CHAPTER TWO

The Business Lunch

Thirteen Simple Rules for the Business Gourmet

THE MAINSTAY of the expense account society is the business lunch. There are business dinners and even a rather reprehensible trend toward business breakfasts (I always brush my teeth after breakfast and find business breakfasts awkward. What do you tip the washroom attendant?), but the business lunch remains the most popular ritual.

The reasons are fairly obvious. You have to eat lunch out during the work day, so why not have the company pay for it? The extended lunch is on company time, while breakfast or dinner would be on what is normally your own time. Thus, both economics and custom weigh in favor of lunch.

The IRS has a more lenient attitude toward business meals than it does toward other business entertainment. For business entertainment there must be "substantial" business discussions, or other mitigating circumstances, to qualify for tax-deductibility. A business meal simply requires a business relationship and a setting "conducive to" business discussion.

There doesn't even have to be any business discussion; although some business is likely to come up no matter how hard you try to avoid it.

As in any ritual, there are rules that should be followed if one hopes to become a successful practitioner of the art of hosting and being hosted at a business lunch:

1. The party paying for the lunch is entitled to choose the restaurant and do most of the talking (if he or she would rather listen, that is also a prerogative of the host).

Exception: If the buyer gives you a choice of locations and the relationship is heavily weighted in your direction—e.g., you're his only customer and without your business, he'd be waiting on tables instead of buying lunches—just pick any place you like and damn the expense. If the relationship is more evenly balanced—you need him nearly as much as he needs you—then be a little more considerate, and, indeed, be careful because you might wind up at the wrong end of the ritual check shuffle.

2. Always make an effort to pick up the check.

This doesn't mean that you will ever have to pay it (at worst, your company instead of his company would pay). The strength of the check-paying effort is inversely proportional to the center of gravity of the business relationship. If he needs you considerably more than you need him, you can make a serious stab at picking up the check. You can grab it and scream and even make a scene. Don't worry. He'll end up paying the check. If, however, the relationship is more evenly balanced—say a seller with a hot product is entertaining you, a buyer who pays cash—care is in order. In this case, you might wave your hand in the direction of the check and mumble something like, "Why don't you let me take it this time?" Don't pick it up, mind you. Just wave at it slowly, as though you were trying to catch an arthritic fly. The instant your companion says, "That's OK, I'll take it," all discussion about the check should come to an abrupt halt. Even another weak wave might invite disaster.

3. Encourage reciprocal relationships, but don't call the lunches "reciprocal."

The best business relationships are those that are evenly balanced. On the surface it may appear that as an entertainee, the more indebted the entertainor, the better. He'll take you to better places and spend more money. That's true, as far as it goes, but is a shortsighted approach. Since there should be some business justification for the lunch, if there is a nice balance of mutuality—he needs your business and you need his product—you can easily develop a symbiotic arrangement: You take him out once and the next time he takes you, and so on. This approach can be expanded into the multisymbiotic lunch, a kind of round-robin. A group of four or five, all of whom have some business dealings with each other, might meet regularly, and each time, a different member of the group picks up the check. This provides ongoing sustenance as long as your company is prepared to go along with a three-figure tab once every four or five weeks.

I should warn you at this point that the tax people do not regard "reciprocal" meals as deductible. However, they do recognize that the practice is widespread and extremely difficult to monitor. If someone takes you to lunch because he's trying to sell you a load of his copper but some months later there's a run on copper and you take him to lunch in an effort to get a little more of the metal than was allotted to you, who can say each did not have clear business purpose? Maybe the IRS.

Anyhow, for the record, this is what the agency has to say about reciprocity: "Frequently, a group of business acquaintances take turns picking up each other's entertainment checks without regard to whether any business purposes are served. These expenses are not deductible."

That particular paragraph deals with entertainment, a

category separate from business meals. Regarding meals, the IRS says, "Business meals furnished to an individual under circumstances generally considered conducive to a business discussion may be deducted, but so-called reciprocal meals may not."

Gratitude runs a close second to greed in the range of human responses, and while the IRS may try to legislate away the urge to reciprocate a kindness, my money is on humanity over bureaucracy.

4. Always take your guest or guests to a restaurant where you're known.

No business luncher worth his American Express card will ever go to a restaurant where he is not greeted by name. It is also a nice touch to choose a place where the maitre d' speaks with a French or Italian accent (French is preferable, but Italian is quite acceptable). It's amazing how important a simple name like Robinson can sound when mispronounced by a tuxedoed Frenchman who appears overwhelmed that you deigned to set foot in his humble, overpriced establishment.

It's no problem getting this kind of greeting. A crisp, green, expense account, tax-deductible bill (actually it doesn't have to be crisp, but should be charged to your company) placed discreetly in the hand of the accented one, on your first few visits, will soon separate you from the anonymous masses. To be sure the maitre d' learns your name, ask him his. Then tell him yours, and reinforce his memory by giving him your business card. And remember, you're *Mr.* Robinson and he's Oscar or Ernest or Andre or Luigi. If this seems a throwback to the old upstairs-downstairs social structure, and alien to the American way of life and the Declaration of Independence, it is. But if you want to play the game, you must obey the rules. It is a game, and Ernest or Luigi knows it and will respect you as one professional to another. Furthermore, when lunch hour is over and Luigi and his cohorts are getting ready for the next seating, you are more likely to be referred to as "that schmuck Robinson" than as *Mr.* Robinson. So don't feel guilty.

On the question of being recognized, the good maitre d' will make every effort to know his customers and greet them by name. It's another way of assuring continued patronage. Paul DeLisle, the genial maitre d' at Washington's San Souci restaurant, takes a professional pride in the ability to recall the names of all his regular customers. "It's strange," he says, "that when I see these people in the streets they look familiar, but I can't remember who they are. But once they walk through the door into my restaurant, I can immediately put a name to the face."

5. Always make a reservation.

Even if you know the restaurant well and find nothing but a vast expanse of white tablecloths every time you go, call ahead. A reservation will help the maitre d' remember who you are, and, at the same time, you can be sure that the restaurant is open. Restaurants that feature empty tables are notoriously bankruptcy prone. Also, some places are closed Mondays or Tuesdays or whatever, a detail easily overlooked in the press of business. Making an appointment to meet someone at a restaurant that is closed or out of business will not create a great deal of good will for your company.

Another thing, even a restaurant that is normally slow can run into an office party or a meeting of the Birdwatchers of America. This can mean a long wait for a table, followed by service that will run from spotty to nonexistent. It is on just such an occasion that you are apt to run into what is known in the trade as the dark-side-of-the-moon strategy. This is a technique designed to assure the customer that whenever he tries to get the attention of a waiter, busboy, or whomever, that person's back will be turned. Eye contact is avoided at all costs, and the more experienced the waiter, the more polished the execution.

What about those establishments that take reservations and then keep you waiting anyhow? I remember a particularly unpleasant experience at a high-priced fish place in Midtown New York. I was hosting a potential news source who could have been extremely valuable to me, and I wanted everything to go right. I picked the place because it was convenient to my guest's office and carefully called for a 12:30 reservation, which was accepted with thanks.

When I arrived at the restaurant (on time), the tables were all occupied and there was a huge crush of humanity straining against the tape, trying to attract the attention of the maitre d', who stood by calmly, calling the names of a favored few. In the midst of this angry mob stood my guest, a small mild-looking fellow, with an expression on his face somewhere between advanced anxiety and sheer panic. I muscled my way through to him and managed to steer him to the small bar in the hope that I could settle his nerves and make him reasonably comfortable while I argued with the captain. The bar was three deep, and the wait for a drink would have been as long as the wait for a table. I got nowhere with the maitre d', who insisted that all these people had reservations ahead of mine, and I would just have to wait or go elsewhere. Half an hour later, drained and irritable, we were seated.

The logical ending to this little story should be that I never heard from this fellow again and blew thirty-five dollars of my company's money for lunch. Actually, he has been pretty helpful, but the restaurant never heard from me again. The care and treatment of restaurants that take but don't honor reservations: avoid them.

6. Don't talk business until the dessert arrives, or, if you don't eat dessert, wait for the coffee.
This is probably better classified as a suggestion than as a rule, but there are some logical reasons to pay attention: (1) if you start talking business before lunch and you see things are going badly, it will ruin your appetite; (2) during the meal, if you chose wisely, you should be fully occupied talking about the flavor of the sauce or the delicacy of the wine, and there would be no time for shop talk; (3) by the time the coffee has

arrived, you and your luncheon companion or companions should be sufficiently relaxed, and so tired of all the small talk, that a gutsy business discussion is likely to be not only acceptable, but even welcome.

Before going on to the next rule, I'd like to pause a moment to discuss a few of the by-products of the expense account business. There are two occupational hazards in working the scene too intensively: obesity and alcoholism.

A bank lending officer I know, who began very early in life to entertain customers and prospects at lunch (I think he invented the three-martini lunch), is now near retirement, and the grind has taken its toll. Every day he would sit at the same table at an exclusive luncheon club and start by belting down two martinis. These would loosen him up, and he would nurse another through lunch to maintain his edge. He was charming and witty and quite successful in attracting new business and expanding existing business.

Thirty years later, he still occupies the same table at the same luncheon club and still downs his two martinis before lunch. But now he often sits alone; and, when he does manage to attract an unwitting guest, he starts his monologue immediately after his first couple of sips and doesn't stop until the last crumb is cleared from the tablecloth. His speech is thick and his subject matter irrelevant and his style rambling and painfully boring: "*I* remember in 1934. . . . *I* was the first. . . . *I* made this branch what it is today. . . . *I* know more about banking than these Harvard MBAs will ever learn. . . . *I* remember when bankers were really bankers. . . . *I* can smell a good loan. . . . *I* never got the money *I* deserved. . . . *I* can run rings around these snot-nosed kids. . . ." You know what I mean. Amputate his first person singular and the entire meal could proceed in merciful silence.

Be forewarned. First, don't get sucked into sitting through one of those interminable sessions. A luncheon invitation from left field should always be checked out. Who is this guy and what does he want of me? If you find yourself putting away a couple drinks every day and you can't get through a business lunch without them, you've got a problem. Try a glass of white wine instead of a cocktail. If your companion doesn't drink, try joining him in not drinking. Don't wind up with a head full of alcohol-soaked mush.

At the same time, the ability to handle a cocktail or two and perhaps some wine at lunch without getting raucous or putting the bread basket on your head is helpful in creating a certain rapport in business relationships. There is no question that alcohol is relaxing and can make even a dull companion seem bearable. The trick is to see that your drinking is under control. Don't have a boozy lunch if you expect a busy or mind-taxing afternoon. Advanced paper-shuffling is about all you can realistically expect to do following the much-maligned three-martini lunch. But if you can arrange your schedule for a light afternoon and you have an important client who thrives on liquid lunches, do it—but not too often.

Now about the weight problem. As a keen observer of business lunchers, I have noticed that most fat people at lunch eat cottage cheese, lettuce, watercress, and black coffee. This led me to conclude that cottage cheese, lettuce, watercress, and black coffee must be extremely fattening. However, upon further investigation, I discovered that fat people order this dreary fare to keep from getting fatter. It is saddening in the extreme to witness a dreadful waste of corporate assets on rabbit food—which, incidentally, costs as much as real food at most expense account restaurants. A little planning will help prevent this waste.

I'm neither a doctor nor a diet specialist, but I know what I see. Aside from a lot of high-calorie booze, the biggest calorie contributor seems to be the bread. That basket of assorted rolls with lots of butter appears on the table almost as soon as you are seated, and while you're talking and waiting, it's there for the nibbling. Unless you're just an occasional luncher, don't touch that stuff. On your birthday you can have one bread-stick, but that's it. I have seen people empty a basket within minutes and call for seconds. Bad news. These are the same people who in a few years are eating lettuce and watercress.

Another major contributor to America's spreading midsection is dessert. The courage required to turn down the *mousse chocolat* at La Caravelle or the pecan pie with whipped cream at the Coach House is something far beyond what is normally assigned to mere mortals. Okay, a couple of times a year, do it. But for the rest of the time, no desserts! Which brings us to the next two rules:

7. *Order a main course, salad (try lemon juice instead of dressing), and coffee. No bread except on your birthday and no dessert except world-renowned dishes twice a year (three times a year if you skip the breadstick on your birthday).*

8. *Watch the booze and check yourself occasionally to determine your degree of dependency.*

There might be a rule somewhere about the optimum length of a business lunch, but the best I can come up with is that it shouldn't be too short or too long. That's about as sneaky a copout as you'll find anywhere. Okay, let's get a little more specific. To start with, a proper business lunch must last more than an hour. You must make it clear that you are important enough not to be constrained by the one-hour-for-lunch policy applicable to the disadvantaged, expense-accountless, working classes. To make this point, you must take "substantially" longer than an hour. Five or ten minutes would not qualify as "substantial" and might even leave the impression that you're a small time, lunch hour cheat. An extra half-hour would suffice to establish you as a person clearly above the average working stiff.

At the other end of the time spectrum, you could be overdoing it if you go beyond two hours. There must be a situation by situation analysis once you pass the obligatory hour-and-a-half. Does your guest have another appointment? Do you have to get back to work? Is the discussion becoming repetitious? Is the conversation flagging? Are there long awkward silences? Dragging out a luncheon beyond any constructive discussion can create the impression that you're just malingering and using the expense account to avoid going back to work. You have a responsibility to maintain the image of the BLs (business lunchers) as a vital part of the American business scene. Don't screw it up for the rest of us.

9. If you're having lunch with your boss (on the company), let him order first.

This gives you a cue to the amount of money he's prepared to spend. If he orders the lobster or the steak or whatever the restaurant's top-of-the-line is, your worries are over. Enjoy yourself. But if he opts for the baked macaroni, be on your guard. You don't have to order macaroni, but stay away from the Chateaubriand. This assumes that you like your job and want to keep it. If your goal is to irritate the ass off the cheap son-of-a-bitch, then you don't need any advice. Just follow your own nasty instincts.

Speaking of cheap sons-of-bitches: an advertising man I know was invited to lunch by his boss, a member of an old-line family with lots of old money, and wound up at a neighborhood luncheonette. Not only that, but when my friend requested that his hamburger be enhanced with a slice of American cheese, the tycoon pointedly explained that the cheese "was ten cents extra." Refusing to be intimidated, my friend went through with his order for a cheeseburger and the old geezer paid the check without further protest. What did the advertising executive learn from the experience? Cheese costs ten cents extra.

Another problem when eating with your boss is the matter of ordering drinks. If the boss orders a double martini, that's carte blanche for you. But if he orders a Virgin Mary or Perrier, better go easy. A glass of white wine may hit just the right note between obsequiousness and latent alcoholism.

10. Be on time.

While there are some who think it's chic to be late for a

luncheon appointment, thus creating the impression that you're a very busy person and are squeezing your lunch companion into a tight schedule, I think it's just bad manners. There is nothing I can think of that is deadlier than sitting at a table alone, nursing a cocktail, and feeling that everyone else in the room is wondering why that poor schnook can't find someone to eat with.

After a few minutes I begin to wonder whether it's the right place or the right day, and finally, if the wait goes beyond ten minutes, I start worrying about how I can justify, for expense account purposes, a meal alone in a three-star restaurant.

If you really have a busy schedule and are unavoidably delayed, at least call or have your secretary call and let your guest (or host) know you're going to be late.

11. Avoid bullshit ploys like having yourself paged or taking phone calls at the restaurant.

You may think that this will impress your guest with your importance, but it's just as likely to convince him that you're grandstanding, even if the interruptions are legitimate. If you're having lunch with someone, you should make every effort to avoid outside distractions.

12. Don't table hop.

Bouncing around a restaurant greeting friends and casual acquaintances may be good for your ego, but leaving your companion to sit around with egg on his face is hardly anybody's idea of creating an atmosphere conducive to business discussion.

13. Finally, if you're host, always pay the hat check charge for your guest.

Even if he or she makes a sincere effort to pay, be firm. It's only a half-dollar or so, but failure to make that final, little gesture can blow the benefits of a forty-dollar luncheon check.

Women and Expense Accounts

Coping with the Corporate Cornucopia

SEVERAL YEARS AGO a committee of the National Organization for Women (NOW) was having a business lunch at a San Francisco hotel. There were seven women and one man at the table.

When the time came for the check, the waitress was at a loss. She knew that the group was militantly feminist, yet all her experience told her that she should give the check to the male. The committee was aware of the waitress's dilemma but made no move to give her direction.

After a period of embarrassed vacillation, the waitress finally dropped the check in front of the male and made a hasty exit. There was much laughter at the table, and when it subsided the ritual began. The check was settled up the way women have been doing these things for generations. Everyone figured out what she (and the one he) had eaten. Then they worked out the mathematics for the tax and the fifteen percent tip, and within fifteen minutes or so each was able to make a pro rata contribution to a pile of bills in the center of the table, and the check was paid.

At about the same time in New York three businessmen were having lunch at one of the classier expense account restaurants considered conducive to business discussion. They ordered drinks, seafood cocktails, and a bottle of fine Bordeaux wine (Mouton Rothschild '73) to go with their carefully aged steaks. They each had a Remy Martin cognac with coffee. When the check came, one businessman snatched it up saying, "Let me take it. I'm in the 70 percent tax bracket, so it'll only cost me thirty cents on the dollar."

The second businessman grabbed it away, insisting that he pay the check: "I'm on an expense account. It won't cost me a penny."

The third businessman snared the check and settled the argument: "Listen fellas, let me pay it. I have a cost-plus contract with the government and if I pay, I'll make some money on it."

The first anecdote is true. The second, I'm not so sure about. But they clearly illustrate the difference in attitudes of men and women, and the NOW story also points up the problem of who pays when there are men and women around—a problem that looms large as women increasingly join the expense account set.

There was a time, not too long ago, when no gentleman would sit by while a woman picked up a check. This would have been the moral equivalent of public castration. The world has changed, but there remains, at least among men over thirty, a residual reluctance to be taken out by a woman, even in a pure business context.

When a man and woman enter a restaurant together, the maitre d', or captain, or whoever greets the couple, will almost invariably play to the man. When the check comes, it's generally placed in front of the man. In fact, a woman executive told me that she wasn't even able to tip a maitre d' on one occasion because he completely ignored her out-stretched hand.

"It seemed to me," she said, "that he was prepared to kiss my hand if I kept it out long enough, but he certainly wasn't going to take any money from me. As a result, we ended up with a table near the men's room."

This woman also found that she never knew how much to tip the captain (in most expense account restaurants the maitre d' is the guy with the foreign accent who greets you at the door, the captain is the smooth-looking chap who takes your order, the waiter is the poor fellow who actually brings the food, and the busboy is the person at the bottom of the heap who cleans up the tables). "It's easy to tip the waiters," she continued. "In New York the sales tax is eight percent; so I just double the tax and the waiters seem perfectly happy. But what do you tip the captain? Two dollars? Five? Ten?

This is not an isolated case. Another lady executive I know flew into a panic when she was entertaining another woman at lunch and the American Express slip came with two spaces for tips; one said "waiter" and the other, "captain." Neither she nor her guest knew what to do; so she rushed to the phone and called her office for instructions. Her boss advised her to give the waiter fifteen percent and the captain five percent. This, incidentally, is the going rate.

While male pride may be one of the cultural roadblocks in the path of women fully realizing their expense account potential, their own readiness to cater to that pride and their own reluctance to give up some of the old feminine preroga-tives continue to retard women's progress. Too many women are prepared to say, "If he wants to pay, I let him. That's his problem." Or, as one attractive vice-president told me, "I'm always wined and dined. The only time I ever pick up a check is when I'm entertaining a woman. Men always pay for me, even if I invite them out."

Because women have been on the receiving end of business

entertainment for so long, some even have difficulty paying for other women. The editor of a retailing magazine told me of her experience:

> I don't have any trouble with men. It's the women who give me a hard time. One particular incident sticks in my mind. I was invited to lunch by a department store executive who spent the entire time pitching a story to me about a merchandising breakthrough at her store. She was quite animated until the check came. Then she seemed to have been struck with a form of selective paralysis. The only thing that still worked was her mouth. She kept talking and talking, but never made a move for the check. As time passed and my deadline crept closer, I had to pick it up myself.

Women who fail to properly assess the business balance of power in any given situation are undermining the very foundations of the expense account and ignoring its rationale. The ultimate purpose of any business-entertainment expenditure is to do something nice for someone in a business relationship so that he/she will do something nice for you. It's that simple.

And speaking of doing something nice for people you do business with, how do women fend off amorous advances in business relationships? For the answer to this, I went to a young, advertising-space salesperson who has a fashion-model figure and face to match, and admits that propositions from male clients are a reality to be dealt with:

> What I try to do, right up front, is to come on real strong businesswise. I bring a lot of material with me, do my homework on his business, and generally make sure early on that I know what I'm talking about and that he knows I'm not trying to get by on my looks. If I begin to suspect that I'm dealing with a lover, I then make it clear that I'm deeply involved with someone and that my business life is distinctly separate from my personal life.
>
> I also try to avoid creating a situation that will encourage a

pass. For instance, I avoid dinners with clients so the question of taking me home doesn't come up. Usually when I take someone to lunch, I'll reserve a quiet table where we can talk. But if I think a guy is going to make a move, I'll book a restaurant that's crowded. You know, where the people at the next table are practically sitting in your lap. This will usually discourage any overtures. Finally, if he persists, I tell him what a terrific guy he is and how I'd love to get to know him better, but that it just doesn't work in a business relationship. "If you get another job or if I get fired, then give me a call."

I really believe that there's nothing to be gained from getting intimately involved with clients. Sure, you'll get a couple of more pages of advertising, but people at the level I deal with aren't stupid. They'll advertise in my publication if they think it pays them to advertise and not because they're sleeping with one of the salespeople. When you're talking about thousands of dollars in ad money, that's too high a price to pay for a roll in the hay.

If some men have a tendency to confuse business romance with personal passion, as a group they are perceived by women as being much more sophisticated in the use of expense accounts than their female counterparts. Women feel that men are more secure and are not in the least bit backward about running up questionable charges. A public relations lady gave me the following example at lunch one day:

> One of the men in my office charged the company for a Mark Cross attaché case. He reasoned that his old attache case was worn out on business and it was rightfully the company's obligation to get him a new one.
>
> The company bounced the chit back and wouldn't pay, but the point is that the man had the brass to ask for it. I think women often don't even charge for expenses that they would be legitimately entitled to. It's probably that they're afraid to be made to appear foolish, so they'd rather just pay themselves.

Conditioning is another important factor that has retarded women from progressing as rapidly as they should in the use of expense accounts. *Working Woman,* a magazine written for women, by women, carried an article (November 1978) in which a clinical psychologist explained the problem in terms of guilt and power. While personally I think this is a lot of bullshit, on the slim possibility that there may be some truth involved, here's what the fellow says: Women equate money with power and have been conditioned not to flash this power around or they will scare men away. He also says something about women feeling guilty about spending money because their mothers never spent any. In essence, he says that women are conditioned to be cheap, and that even if they come into large sums of money, they continue to be cheap.

How will this be overcome? "As increasing numbers of women work and begin to recognize their financial independence and individual worth, the money-power play will change," says *Working Woman,* paraphrasing the good psychologist. Women will begin to see themselves as equals to male colleagues, they will gain more confidence, and they won't "have to demonstrate vulnerability through a show of poverty."

In the meantime, working women are advised to do a little self-analysis, to try to discover the real reasons behind their actions, and to decide honestly whether they want to continue being cheap or are prepared to change.

In another article, *Working Woman* gets closer to the heart of the matter and urges women to cast off some of their old notions about spending money. The article cites a public relations firm, owned and run by females, which was found to charge clients considerably less for expenses than other, presumably male-dominated, public relations firms. Furthermore, the magazine pointed out, ninety percent of the members of the New York Society of Association Executives, most of whom are men, charged association dues to their companies, while only about half of the members of the Financial Women's Association of New York charged their dues. These examples indicate clearly (at least to *Working Woman*) that men make better use of expense accounts than women.

I think a better indication of the naiveté of women when dealing with expense accounts is a question posed in the article: "What if your best friend works for a company that just completed a business deal with your firm—can you take her to lunch at company expense?"

The answer, by a woman, to a woman: "That might be pushing things, but if you think your lunch could augment the business side of your friendship and lead to future deals, under the IRS guidelines for meals it could be a valid expense."

If a man were asked that same question, the answer would be much less self-conscious. Something like, "You bet your ass, honey, and if you like, take her to dinner and a show."

Women, the magazine says, tend to look at expense accounts the way they look at household budgets—so much money coming in and so much going out. Forget that (*Working Woman* says); expense accounts are different. "The more you spend, the more your company may make."

I'm not sure that that logic is ironclad, but it's a good start. Expense accounts are a recognized cost of doing business, and women should get over being self-conscious about spending the boss's money, even at times when the benefits to the business appear nebulous. It's all part of a mysterious process called "profit maximization."

Step one for a woman looking for the joys of expense account living is to get the kind of job that provides expenses over and above petty cash for coffee and postage stamps. Just about any sales position calls for T&E expenditures, but some firms pay the expenses of salespersons, while others deduct it from commissions. In the long run, the net result is the same. A company will not continue to pay the expenses of a salesperson who doesn't generate commissions. But, as we all know, in the long run we're all dead; so for the short run, look for a company that picks up expenses. You'll be a lot more comfortable, and perhaps more effective, if you feel you're spending the company's money rather than your own.

Employment areas, in addition to selling, that provide expense accounts are much too numerous to list, but a few that come quickly to mind are public relations, lobbying, advertising, publishing, retailing, and banking. Perks are also available as women move up in the corporate hierarchy, but I don't think women executives will have any more trouble utilizing a company-paid penthouse than a male executive; so I'll deal with that subject on a nondiscriminatory basis.

Step number two involves getting the most mileage out of an expense account by learning to use it properly. And since, for the moment at least, most of the people you will be trying to influence will probably be male, it behooves you to consider male feelings.

Although the male's reticence about being treated by a female is fading, it has not disappeared. The male is still prone to pay for the female under business circumstances that, all things being equal, would dictate that the female pay. Here is an instance:

A public relations person, by definition, is one who buys lunch for newspeople. There may be some other functions involved in PR, but I'm sure they aren't terribly important. Yet I have on occasion committed the unspeakable act of picking up a check for a PR person. Needless to say, that PR person was never a male person, always a female person.

An apparel manufacturer in my set is a large advertiser in a number of trade papers and magazines, and is often entertained by ad salespersons and publishers. The relationships are such that he is the entertainee and they are the entertainors.

"I have no reason to reciprocate," he says, "because they're after my business. But when I'm taken out by women, I somehow find myself picking up the check. I guess it's conditioning. It's not that I never let a woman pay for me. I do. But if it were a man buying, I would never think of taking the check."

Women should be strong enough and secure enough to

evaluate their positions vis-à-vis their companions' positions on the same basis that men do, and should not be tempted to capitulate to male pride. Even under extreme circumstances, hold your ground.

A very attractive securities analyst (the analyst, not securities) tells of taking out a large institutional customer:

> [He was] much older than I and a singularly unattractive looking man. I could feel the eyes of other people in the restaurant staring at us and could hear snatches of conversation along the lines of "What's that young, pretty girl doing with that ugly old man. . . . He must really be loaded," and that sort of thing.
>
> Then when the meal was over and I picked up and paid the check, I think half the people in the place nearly choked on their soufflés.

That's what I mean. If you're supposed to entertain in business, don't be put off by outside pressure. If the lady had been the least bit self-conscious and had hesitated for an instant about paying, there's no question that the ugly old man would have taken the tab. But when it came to buying that big block of stock that her company was trying to unload, he might remember that nice young man at another investment firm who took him to dinner a week earlier . . . and *paid*.

Until the last vestige of the male role as a hunter and provider is swept away, a woman who wants to get the most business benefit from expense account entertainment should maintain an aura of professionalism and at the same time remain sensitive to the feelings of her companion (male).

Credit cards are a must, and the woman who is doing the entertaining should check beforehand to be sure that the card she carries is honored by the restaurant she chooses. Even the most liberated of males would find it somewhat uncomfortable to sit by while a woman dug through her bag to count out cash. If this has been further complicated by the woman's effort to use a credit card in a place that doesn't accept credit cards, or a Master Charge where only American Express is honored, the entire entertainment effort can go down the drain.

If there is an ego problem when with a man being taken to dinner one-on-one by a woman, consider the plight of a man who goes along when his executive wife is taking out a client and spouse. It's one thing for a man to get a fish eye from a waiter or captain he'll never see again, but it's another to sit by while another couple watches your wife pick up the check and generally run things at what looks like a social evening but is really a business meeting.

If the executive wife permits her husband to do all the honors and then pays him back in the privacy of their home (and gets reimbursed by her company) it creates an ambiguous situation for the client. He doesn't know for sure whether the lady executive's company or her husband is footing the bill. This could lead to a big fuss about who is paying what and could embarrass everybody.

One solution is to have everything arranged in advance so that either the wife or the company gets billed after the fact and the question of who is paying the check just doesn't come up. If it does, the wife can simply say "the company is taking care of everything," and that should end the discussion.

It's important for the woman executive to at least make an effort to gauge the sensitivity of a male entertainee. For the most sensitive, a private club where only members can run up charges makes it very clear who is the host and who is the guest. The club provides a comfortable rationalization for the guest: "I would never allow a woman to pay for me, but what can I do? I'm not a member." There are still some clubs that don't permit women members, but their number is dwindling, and if current trends continue there will be damned few clubs able to survive without the revenue from women on expense accounts.

Another male ego-saver used by some women is to sign a

credit card receipt in blank and leave it to the restaurant to fill it out after the meal is over. The waiter will even write his own tip at whatever percentage you advise. The charge is then mailed to you or to your company, and the mundane matter of money never arises. Your guest knows who's paying, and you know, but the guy at the next table doesn't. Of course, this arrangement can be used only at a restaurant where you are well known and that is well known to you. The opportunity for bill-padding is obvious, but most restaurant keepers know where their bread is buttered and will not jeopardize a continuing relationship by jerking around the numbers.

As I mentioned before, men are slowly beginning to adjust to the new order, and many will not be the least bit disturbed if the lady pays the bill, as long as it's done efficiently and in a matter-of-fact style. Here is one veteran lunch buyer's method:

> Normally, when I invite a client to lunch, I call the restaurant in advance, ask for a nice table, and make it clear that I'll be paying the check. At some point during the meal, I'll excuse myself to go to the ladies room and take the opportunity to sign an American Express slip in blank.
>
> I'll tell the waiter to fill it in, add a twenty percent tip, and mail the slip to my office with a copy of the itemized check. The client is completely relaxed.
>
> I recognize male pride and certainly don't want to embarrass a client. That is, most of the time I don't. Once in a while I run into one of those real male chauvinist bastards, and just to puncture his ego, I'll have the check brought to me and I'll make a big production of paying it.
>
> I'll add up the numbers slowly, maybe call the waiter over to check an item or two; then I'll shove a couple of plates around a little so I can get comfortable signing the credit card voucher. All this time, I can feel the son-of-a-bitch squirming. I know it's not a good way to promote my business, but sometimes it's worth it just for the satisfaction.

The first time I was treated to lunch by a woman who was

not my mother, it was a traumatic experience. I was so concerned about what I was going to do when the check came that my conversation flowed like a dry creek, and even a double scotch failed to loosen me up. The food seemed to stick in my throat, and I soaked through a new handkerchief in a vain effort to keep my forehead dry. The lady did her best to put me at ease, but with little success. When the check came, she took firm command of it, presenting her credit card and signing with no nonsense, and it was all over. What the hell was I so worried about?

Having survived a kind of gastronomic deflowering, I can now be pretty cool, but I still have trouble with the amateur accountants who work over the figures as though preparing a certified audit. While the lady is subtracting the pinky and adding the thumb, I can almost hear the waiter mumbling that if I were half a man I'd pay the fucking check so he could go on to the next table.

In the case of the lady who deliberately sets out to give her chauvinist guest the business, it's forgivable. But when it's mathematical ineptitude or a form of paranoia (all waiters are cheats and all restauranteurs are members of the Mafia), the professional polish that we all strive for can be totally dissipated.

Sure, waiters make mistakes, but these are as likely to be in your favor as in theirs. Know the place you are going and the prices they charge. After a couple of trips, it's fairly easy to know, within a dollar or two, what the check should be. If it looks out of line, find out why. If not, pay the money and get on with it. It's not your money anyhow.

There's another good reason for knowing the prices a restaurant charges. Since many corporations have limits on how much they'll pay for an expense account meal, you'd better be sure that the place you choose is within the allowable range. Don't be like a woman executive for an insurance company who took an analyst out to dinner and was hit with a ninety dollar check. Her company had a fifty dollar limit on this type of dinner, and she couldn't even get that much because she had no documentation for the below-fifty-dollar expenditure. She had to pay the ninety dollars out of her own pocket.

Again, turning to my own experience, I think women could become much more relaxed about using expense account money to its full potential if they would just think of it as another charge account at Bloomingdales. Forget all that crap about guilt and power and vulnerability, and spend what you can, always keeping in mind that the expenses are for "ordinary and necessary business purposes" and will produce maximum profits for your company and some very comfortable living for you.

The women who have been brought up in the expense account society have honed their techniques to the same sharpness as their male counterparts. A publishing executive I interviewed told me she considers herself at least on a par with the males at her job level: **2068534**

> I've had an expense account since I was a pup. Early in my career I worked as a bureau chief for one of the national news magazines and had to deal with travel expenses on assignments. You can be sure that when I was on a trip, I didn't eat at McDonalds. I stayed at the best hotels and ate at the bèst restaurants. When I was transferred to New York as a senior editor, I found that there was a kind of competition and heavy expense account activity was expected. It was part of the office politics. The more charges you ran up, the more important you became. I had no problem joining in the game.
>
> My job now involves developing story ideas and working with free-lance writers. I'm quite comfortable taking male writers to lunch. It's an editor-writer relationship, and gender doesn't enter into it. Writers love to be taken out to lunch.

I'm confident that given time, opportunity, and experience women will outperform men in the expense account game by a couple of light years. I should know. I'm the guy who pays all those bills at Bloomingdales.

CHAPTER FOUR

The Practical Side

Peer Pressure and the Phantom at the Table

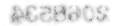

AMONG THE MOST DIFFICULT TASKS confronting the expense account set is the appraisal of associates to determine how much to spend, on whom, and how often. There are a number of variables which must be factored in, and there cannot be any hard rules to fit every situation. But generally, here are the questions to ask yourself:

- How much can your company afford?
- How much will your company tolerate?
- How important are you within your organization?
- How often will you be entertaining this person?
- What are the prevailing standards of entertainment in your community and in your business?

The answer to the first question is crucial, but fairly easy to ascertain. Most employees have a pretty good idea of the profitability of the firms they work for. If figures aren't released publicly, reliable estimates can be obtained at the water cooler or the Xerox machine or, if you really want solid information, the rest rooms. If your company is doing well, the chances are it will not be overly sensitive to a little extravagance on the expense account. If it is having a bad time, don't compound its problems with unnecessary and excessive expenditures. Change jobs.

Heavy expense account outlays at a company that is having financial problems are self-defeating. Expense account abuses at Weeden and Company, a once powerful Wall Street investment firm, were said to have been a major contributor to the company's decline. One of the company's top officers reportedly turned in nearly $200,000 in expense account charges over a six-year period and wound up out of his job and, according to an account in *Institutional Investor* (June 1978), agreed to sign promissory notes to repay at least part of the $200,000. The magazine also reported that liberal expense accounts were one of the major attractions at the company, quoting a stock trader as stating, "A lot of people justified being there because of the expense accounts. I mean, where else could you get paid a salary you could live with plus have an expense account of $20,000 or so?"

Assuming your company is comfortably profitable, it then becomes necessary to determine how much expense account living it will tolerate. Some corporations have clear guidelines on expenses they will allow various levels of employees, and very tight reporting requirements. For instance, Boeing Corporation—awash in billion dollar contracts, and earning record profits—requires vice-presidents to document such extravagances as bridge tolls and cab fares.

Some guidelines are patently absurd and require a touch of creativity to live within them. If, for instance, a company allows twenty dollars for lunch for two and thirty dollars for three, it has been said that on occasions an employee will spend thirty dollars on lunch for two and add a phantom luncheon companion to comply with company policy. The more sensitive among us might regard this as dishonesty. However, the practice is fairly common and can be easily rationalized thusly: The lunch was legitimately business-oriented; the company has this stupid policy, wholly out-of-tune with prevailing prices, and will be adequately compensated by the good will and business generated by the extra ten bucks.

Your corporate controller may not see it quite that way, so if you ever choose to invite a phantom luncheon companion, be sure of two things: (1) the phantom did not have lunch with your controller or have lunch with someone else in your organization on the same day (nothing can be more awkward than having to explain how the same person ate two lunches at the same time at different places; and (2) the phantom meets the qualifications your company would expect of an entertainee.

In extreme cases, it might make sense to inform the unfed party of his status. Generally, this is not a good idea. You become involved in a conspiracy that could make a big deal of what amounts to a detail. If you get caught, it will be easier to merely explain that what you did was in the company's best interest, and if you still have your job expect your future expenses to be scrutinized unmercifully. And even if you do get away with an occasional phantom, don't make it a habit. Remember friends, moderation in all things, including expense account fudging.

On the question of your importance within your organization, it is hardly worth dwelling on the difference in the expense allowance of the chief executive officer and the third-assistant vice-president. However, in dealing with executives who are on the same level, you will find some spend considerably more than their counterparts. Find out who, and how much, and choose your own role model.

The importance of the person being entertained—his standing within his own company and his company's impact or potential impact on your company's prosperity—is critical in determining how far you can go in running up charges. Nobody at your company is likely to complain if you spend $100 at dinner with the president of your company's best customer or with the head of that company's purchasing department. On the other hand, if you spend that kind of money on an assistant accounts receivable clerk or a minor supplier, trouble could ensue (unless your company is behind in its payments and needs help in keeping supply lines open).

Veterans of the expense account wars have, in the past, awarded battlefield promotions to their luncheon companions when the level of their expenditures appeared to be far above the level of the executive entertained. A low-level executive with high-level taste can be an embarrassment; so, to avoid a hassle when the charge is turned in, an instant promotion might be in order. This device has its dangers and must be used with the same discretion required for phantom lunchers.

Levels of entertainment vary from industry to industry and with the price levels of localities. I remember having lunch in Greenville, South Carolina, with the president of a major public company, at the best restaurant in town. The check came to $6.45 for two. Now, for Greenville, that was a pretty fancy lunch. In New York or San Francisco you could barely get an appetizer for that kind of money. At the Imperial Hotel in Tokyo a meal for two in 1978 came to $100, and both diners left hungry.

Industry standards—what your competitors are doing—must be factored into any expense account formula. An advertising or publishing executive might think nothing of spending seventy-five dollars for lunch at the '21', while the sales manager for a paint supply wholesaler could run into trouble charging five dollars for lunch at McDonalds.

As to the frequency of entertainment, if the same name crops up time after time on your expense reports, be sure you can show good business reasons for meeting so often. Don't press your luck by turning in large chits week after week. Let up once in a while. It will keep the heat off and might even benefit your health. How many times a week can you put up with lobster diablo or prime ribs au jus?

To learn what your company's expense account traffic will bear, ask questions and test the water by gradually increasing your standard of entertaining. Watch for the response. If your boss begins to grumble, back off a bit. If everything goes through smoothly, keep the pressure up, but always remember the need for justification. In the end, to satisfy the IRS, you have to show your company that your expenses are "ordinary, incidental, and job related." And most important, you have to show that your luxurious lifestyle is "maximizing profits."

In handling an expense account, the usual practice is to worry about spending too much and upsetting your boss or the IRS. But there's another possibility—spending too little. Chintzing on expenses when entertaining good customers or prospective customers might be like throwing money down the drain. A second-rate meal at a third-rate restaurant could send your customer scurrying to a competitor, who may not have as good a product, but who knows how to make the customer feel warm.

If you are already getting results, in the form of more business, there is real pressure from your company to keep those entertainment expenses up. If your expenses begin to slip off, your boss is going to worry that you're not doing your job.

One public relations executive who worked for a large insurance company in the Midwest found himself conscience striken because of all the pressure to spend:

> This company thought I was working miracles for them by getting stuff printed, and they were convinced that the whole ballgame was in the T&E. If my expense slips dropped off in even a single week, I'd get some feedback suggesting that I should continue entertaining on the scale that they had become accustomed to. If my expenses were down for a month, I'd get a call from the treasurer himself, telling me quite bluntly to go out more and spend more money. I suspect that the treasurer

was living pretty good on the expense account and wanted to keep my chits up so that his would look better.

Anyhow, I started taking my girl friends out on expenses. Every night we'd go to a different restaurant, the theatre, the works. My entire social life was on the pad. I was drinking too much, eating too much. I think I came pretty close to becoming an alcoholic during that stage. It was a very strange feeling, having to maintain the level of spending to keep them off my back.

Now I'm with an agency and they keep track of expenses with a very sharp pencil. You practically have to fill out an affidavit to buy a bottle of beer for the editor-in-chief of the *New York Times*. And you know something? I'm relieved. Expense account cheating just goes against my nature, but what could I do. I wanted to hold on to my job.

Peer pressure is another fact of expense account life. With a number of colleagues doing the same thing you do, expense accounts must come out with some degree of comparability. A salesman who spends $10,000 a year on T&E and brings in a million dollars worth of business will be compared with another who spends $5,000 and brings in two million. This could mean trouble for the $10,000 a year spender. He will either have to cut down or get the $5,000 a year deadbeat to trade up.

The first major trip I ever took on the expense account was to the West Coast to cover a convention, and I was appalled at the cost of everything. When I got back and started to fill out my expense report, the numbers just seemed out of sight. The hotel bill and plane fare were all clearly documented; so there was nothing I could do about that, but there were meal charges and phone calls and drinks and the like, all of which were estimated. After adding up my first estimates, I was convinced that these charges would never be approved.

I started shaving, and when I got finished, my estimates were below my out-of-pocket expenses, but I figured that even if it cost me a hundred bucks or so, that was pretty cheap for a trip to California and all that luxury living.

When I finally brought the report over to the editor for approval, he looked it over and said, "This is the cheapest tab I've ever seen for a trip to the Coast. What the hell did you do, live on spaghetti and meatballs? The next time I send you out, you'd better spend more money, or you'll ruin it for everyone else in the office."

I left his desk with a sinking feeling in my stomach and a promise to myself that I would never again jeopardize the lifestyle of my colleagues.

Another recurring problem of expense-account living is this: does it make more sense to spend your own money and be reimbursed later by your firm, or to charge business expenses, get your money, and pay the bills later? Based on pure economics, it's smarter to get your money first and pay when the bills come in. You then have the use of your company's money for the time between the reimbursement and the due date of the bills. This could run to a month or two and help you through some cash flow problems.

However, there is a psychological price paid for the additional cash flow. The danger is that once you get your money it will get lost among your general funds, and when the bills come you will be in the same position as those who must struggle without expense accounts: the money gone, and the bills unpaid. There goes your peace of mind.

The decision must be made on an individual basis. If you have the discipline to get early reimbursement and plan carefully to be sure that when the bills come, the money will be available for payment—great. You might even put the money in a day-of-deposit, day-of-withdrawal, interest-bearing savings account and earn a little on your company's money. But if you're one of those weak-willed types who spends it when he gets it and worries later, pay with your own money, and when you get repaid it will feel like a bonus.

The cash flow concept can be pressed further. American Express, for example, expects to be paid as soon as you receive their statement. If you pay anytime before the next month's

THE PRACTICAL SIDE   43

billing period, nobody complains. This gives you nearly thirty days in which to play around with their money. If you don't pay within the thirty days, their computer sends you a little note informing you that the bill is overdue. If you pay during the next billing period, this satisfies the computer, assuming you also pay the charges you ran up in the second billing period. That gives you another thirty days to play around with some of their money.

A very sophisticated financier I know has a corporate policy under which American Express charges are always paid during the second billing period, and since he runs a pretty sizable business, the float (the money due but unpaid) increases his working capital. Caution: Don't try this game with a bank credit card, since they charge interest in the neighborhood of eighteen percent a year and nothing makes the banks happier than slow payers. In fact, Citibank in New York at one time added a fifty cent service charge to the bills of their Master Charge customers who paid on time! However, the bank gave up the practice when its competitors failed to join in the practice of penalizing prompt payers.

In fairness, I would never single out American Express for the cash flow play except for a commercial of theirs which I found particularly offensive. Actor Karl Malden would get on the tube, and with all the sincerity he could muster would advise the public that after returning from a trip financed with American Express travelers checks, one of the checks should be squirreled away indefinitely as "emergency" money. Then, the message went, a quick twenty dollars would always be available in a corner of your wallet or in your shoe if you should find yourself otherwise broke.

What Karl Malden didn't say in the commercial is that the real profit in selling travelers checks is in the float. People buy the checks today, spend them over a period of a week or a month or a year or whatever. In the meantime, American Express has the use of all that cash, which is invested and earns interest for American Express. All those whom the company can convince to hold on to travelers checks indefinitely become investors who get no return on their investment. So remember this, American Express: shrewd cash management is a two-way street.

Once you're in a spot that provides an expense account, some planning is in order to assure that you get your fair share of the T&E money. Normally, corporations allow for T&E in departmental budgets. If you want to get yours, it must be built into the budget, sometimes as much as a year before the fact. If there's a convention you think you would like to attend (for the good of the company, of course), sell the boss on it before the budget is completed.

In fact, if you're really serious in your search for excellent living on other people's money, draw up a budget for yourself. List the meetings and conventions you think you should go to; the people that should be entertained; the type of entertainment that would be appropriate; and traveling you think you should do.

The bottom line should be an estimate of the cost of this program and of the benefit to the business. It's impossible to get realistic figures on the benefits, but don't let that deter you. It's no more difficult than estimating the gross national product or projecting the level of inflation; yet economists do these things all the time, and the rest of us rely on the figures. Your estimate of the benefits will be based on the kind of business you're in, but if you have any problem, just pick a nice round figure that yields a fifteen to one or twenty to one benefit to cost ratio. Then add a big number for good will.

Take this budget in to your boss and be prepared to negotiate. By the time the session is over, you'll probably find that half your suggestions wind up on the cutting room floor, but you will have considerably more than if you had not presented the budget in the first place.

CHAPTER FIVE

Expense Account Abuses

The Port Authority Caper

ABUSES OF EXPENSE ACCOUNTS generally are handled very quietly between the company and the alleged abuser. The purported perpetrator can expect anything from a mild suggestion, such as "go a little easier on expenses," to summary dismissal. If the fraud is blatant enough, it may lead to criminal charges.

One celebrated case was spread all over the front pages. It involved charges of expense account cheating at the Port Authority (PA) of New York and New Jersey, a quasi-public corporation that runs a complex of New York and New Jersey tunnels, airports, bridges, and the twin, 107-story, World Trade Center buildings. The PA is a big money maker and apparently provided its employees liberal expense accounts with rather loose reporting requirements.

An investigation resulted in the indictment of two officials, each of whom was earning more than $50,000 a year. Each was accused of defrauding the PA of more than $1,500 by expense account padding.

The director of public relations was suspended from his job; but, after repaying $1,619.91, he was appointed assistant director at $49,504. He admitted faking expense slips by falsely listing the names of newsmen or public officials as his guests. However, he said, he was only following the accepted practices at the PA. Eventually, he pleaded guilty to reduced charges and paid a $1,000 fine.

One of the investigations leading up to the indictments was conducted by the accounting firm of Coopers and Lybrand, and a report was issued in January of 1978 with details of improprieties and recommendations for tightening up PA's expense account procedures. The accounting firm's report covered the twelve months through July 31, 1977, during which time the PA spent $850,000 on expenses. How much was legitimate and how much fraudulent was not specifically determined, but the report concluded that "a significant number of employees had improper or questionable charges."

Most of the improprieties involved standard expense account ploys—double-dipping and phantom guests. Double-dipping is the practice of submitting two bills for the same expenditure. This can be done by first turning in the tissue paper receipt retained when you charge a meal or other expense with a credit card. Then when the "hard-copy," a cardboard receipt, comes in the mail, it is turned in for a second reimbursement. This procedure is dumb and can be spotted by any employer with decent controls. But where expenses are loosely monitored, the duplicate charges might slip through unnoticed.

A lot of phantom luncheon partners also turned up in the course of the accounting firm's investigation. Investigators called 1,900 of the people listed as entertainees and succeeded in contacting 1,600, of whom 240 could not recall being entertained at the time and place specified on the expense vouchers. From that 240, came various explanations:

- They had never attended the function described in the expense report.
- They didn't even know the PA employee submitting the charge.
- They had been at the function, but were not entertained by the PA employee.
- The meeting was personal and had nothing to do with business.
- They were there, but paid their own way.

There were probably many more than the 240 found by the accountants who were not bona fide guests, but the accountants stopped making calls on an employee's expenses as soon as three phony entries were uncovered. At that point, the employee's name was forwarded to the PA's general counsel for further investigation.

There were also instances of double-eating among senior management personnel: on the same day, charges were entered in their names at the PA dining room and at an outside restaurant. The accountants concluded that one employee must have forged another's signature; although the word "forgery" was carefully avoided.

Abuses involving direct charges from airlines, restaurants, and hotels were also uncovered. These charges were often left out of the expense reports. Furthermore, the accountants discovered that employees authorized to approve these direct charges "were also authorized to create new vendor codes, thereby making it possible for new vendors to be paid via the normal processing of accounts payable system without further approval or review."

The report did not get overly specific on this point, but accountants familiar with corporate controls pointed out that this was an extremely dangerous procedure for any company. An internal controls expert told me, "An employee could set up a nonexistent business, with a letterhead and a bank account, and run monthly bills through the company. These would be paid without any question, and the employee could just pocket the proceeds."

Another leaky area discovered by the investigators of the PA was in the food services division. It was a regular practice for the manager of the division to have cash advances, ranging from $500 to $3,000, outstanding: "Expense reports submitted by this employee listed substantial cash expenditures to five liquor stores and one bakery, aggregating approximately $14,000. The individual charges comprising these purchases (ranging from less than $25 to $1,100) were supported by receipts from the bakery and liquor stores; however, the purpose of the purchases was not set forth on the individual expense reports and was in general only labeled 'refreshments' and 'bakery.'"

There were some employees with "assignments of a sensitive nature" who were not required to submit the names of business guests, the report noted. What type of employees had these "sensitive assignments?" The report didn't say, but some off-the-record investigation pointed to lobbyists who submitted chits that read "lunch with the U.S. Senate" or "dinner with the Navy." The point of these vague descriptions was to avoid embarrassing any individual within the group the lobbyist was seeking to influence.

In the newspaper business I have seen expense slips which list "lunch with a confidential source," and these go through, assuming the numbers are not astronomical. The IRS does permit a certain amount of discretion when it comes to confidential information, but if push comes to shove, all the standard information—who, what, when, where, and why—will have to be made available if a deduction is to be allowed.

Specifically, the IRS says, "Confidential information relating to an element of an otherwise deductible expenditure, such as the place, business purpose, or business relationship, need not be set forth in your account book, diary, or other record if the information is recorded elsewhere at or near the time of the expenditure and is available to fully substantiate that element of the expenditure."

You don't have to tell the whole neighborhood, but if the IRS wants to know, you tell or lose the deduction.

The cash expenditures at the PA on booze and baked goods may also have been used for missions of a sensitive nature. Since the PA is basically a political animal, created by the State of New York and New Jersey, state legislators might look more kindly on the PA's plans and procedures if they were periodically plied with pastries or wooed with vodka. This subject, however, was beyond the scope of the report.

The information uncovered clearly indicated that abuses at the PA resulted from a combination of sloppy controls, an outdated policy with unrealistic spending limits, and greedy employees who took advantage of the system. Maximum charges allowed for hotel rooms were well below the going rate so the maximums were widely ignored. And, in exceeding the unrealistic maximums, lodging charges were "clearly excessive."

Although policy permitted expense reports for under twenty-five dollars to be submitted without documentation, there were "numerous" instances of larger charges coming in undocumented. Moreover, "numerous instances occurred of certain employees consistently charging less than twenty-five dollars for meals, thereby not requiring the submission of supporting receipts." The PA had a formal policy against charging meals one employee bought for another; so employees would list an outside person as the guest, and get paid.

Finally, the report noted that expenses charged for family members accompanying PA employees on trips were not always justified: "In certain instances, due to the nature of the event, it appeared appropriate for wives to accompany their husbands. In such instances reimbursement of the spouse's expenses appeared to be proper."

But, the report continued, there were specific instances in which the PA paid for family expenses which were clearly personal.

Coopers and Lybrand recommended that the PA update its

expense policies to conform with current economic conditions and business practices and put it all in writing. These policies should be reviewed periodically and modified in the light of changing conditions.

Noting that review and control of expenses at the departmental level had been ineffective, the report suggested that expense reports and petty cash vouchers be reviewed by the accounting department. At a minimum, the review should require receipts, identification of guests, and a clear statement of business purpose. Additional recommendations were as follows:

- There should be strict limits on the type of employee services that can be billed directly, and departmental authority to approve open account payments to these vendors should be discontinued. This authority should be limited to the director of finance or the controller. Also, the master file of vendors supplying employee-related goods or services should be reviewed periodically by a responsible employee. (This obviously to avoid the possibility of payments to a dummy supplier.)
- Cash expenditures should be kept to small amounts. "The practice of utilizing cash for significant purchases, including such items as food and beverages, should be discontinued."
- Club memberships should be reviewed and limited to those that are justified in relation to cost.
- Use of the PA-owned dining room should be encouraged over outside restaurants, and dining room charges should be reviewed periodically.
- The expense account reporting system should be segregated by individual in order that an individual's expense record would be easily accessible for monitoring. (The PA system lumped all expense reports together chronologically; as a result, the accountants had to wade through the whole file to follow up on any individual's expense record.)

The publicity, the investigation, and the tightened controls will probably inhibit the expense account life of PA employees, but it is doubtful that this type of investigation will become an everyday exercise for American industry. The cost of the Coopers and Lybrand assignment to the PA was a whopping $400,000. This expenditure resulted in the recovery of a grand total of $10,824 from employees who were caught cheating. That's a pretty steep price to pay to recover what amounts to petty cash.

Most expense account cheating will probably be handled on an *ad hoc* basis, with the punishment designed to fit the crime. A friend who supervises a group of account executives found that three out of four expense slips turned in to him reported the same person being taken to lunch on the same day by three different staff members. Did he scream for the cops or call for an audit? No. He just called them all into his office, handed back the expense slips, and said, "Look fellas, if you're going to fake your expenses, better do a little more efficient job of coordinating. In the meantime, take these back and give me some different names."

CHAPTER SIX

Expense Account Sex

Freeloading in the Erogenous Zones

"IT HAS ALL BEEN ARRANGED." In Japan, this line might follow an evening of expense account entertainment—drinks, dinner, geisha girls smiling and serving sake. Its meaning is clear to anyone familiar with the mysteries of the Orient: your host has rented a hotel room for you, and the geisha who has been giggling at everything you've said, and pressing her hand against your thigh at every opportunity, will spend the night with you. But you don't have to go all the way to Japan for expense account sex. You can get it in New York, Chicago, San Francisco, Miami, in just about any United States city where businessmen gather to sell or buy or rent or talk.

New York has an ample supply of swank apartments, lavishly furnished and fully equipped with models, actresses, or just plain hookers who provide sex for businessmen at prices that virtually mandate expense account money or some other form of corporate financing if the enterprises are to survive. And they do survive. Indeed, they prosper.

An article in *New York Magazine* on "The Best Little Whorehouse in New York" reported that this Park Avenue brothel, with rates of $100 to $200 for a one-hour visit, grossed $1,314,000 a year, and a cool million of that wound up as clear profit. The magazine also explored five other brothels, offering varying degrees of luxury, and found prices ranging from $40 to $70 an hour. These places would surely perish without substantial subsidies from business and, indirectly, from the IRS.

In any business that operates on the fringes of the law, cash (as opposed to checks) is much admired. Cash that is unrecorded and not subject to the clutching fingers of the IRS provides the lifeblood for the better sex palaces and massage parlors in New York City.

The garment business, which is New York's largest employer, is uniquely endowed for generating cash. On Saturdays and Sundays many garment manufacturers open their showrooms to the retail trade, and bargain hunters flock in to buy wholesale. These showroom sales are often made for cash, cash that may never find its way into the records of the seller. Since it's not recorded coming in, it need not be accounted for going out. This creates a convenient reservoir from which cash can be drawn to send buyers to expensive whorehouses or to pay kickbacks or for the owners to live a little more comfortably.

Of course, not all Saturday and Sunday sales are for cash and unrecorded, but enough are to keep the better bordellos operating happily in the black. Marginal retailers often buy for cash and sell for cash, and the money never gets recorded anywhere. Finally, cash can be generated by phony cab fares and other under-twenty-five-dollar items that need not be documented for IRS scrutiny.

Although whorehouses were not among the businesses cited by legislators who expressed concern about the financial hardships that might result from a curtailment of business entertainment, they belong in that category.

The views of the IRS notwithstanding, sex *is* entertainment. And since travel and entertainment remain legitimate business deductions, the word entertainment is often more liberally defined by businesses than by stuffy government agencies.

There is no doubt that the supplying of sexual favors for important clients or customers is fairly commonplace throughout the commercial world, but you'll never see an expense report listing "$100 for a call girl for the sales manager of Acne Screw Works." Instead, sex expenditures are hidden under such general categories as promotional expenses, advertising costs, or simply "entertainment."

Some companies devise elaborate ruses to cover money spent to supply sex. One manufacturer registered his own private madam as an interior decorator. Charges for sex came through on invoices headed "interior decorating services."

A massage parlor in the Wall Street area set up a dummy company as financial consultants and billed clients for "tax consulting services" so as not to rub the IRS the wrong way. Generally, however, expenses for sex are just buried in the T&E account.

Sex in business is not limited simply to providing sexual partners. The range of sexual favors supplied by one business-man for another is broad. It runs from a pretty secretary who agrees to have dinner and perhaps go dancing with an important and lonely client, to hostesses hired to pin name tags on visiting conventioneers, to a call girl in a hotel room, to a full-blown orgy.

Sex can also become a fringe benefit in the normal course of expense account living. As business becomes more coeduca-tional, conventions and sales meetings that were once male dominated have become much more evenly balanced, sex-wise. Since most meetings are at hotels or resorts which furnish a relaxed atmosphere and good food, drinking, and dancing, nature has a way of drawing together persons of different sexual persuasions. Sometimes it requires a lot of persuasion and sometimes not too much, but the incidence of convention-eers sleeping with each other must increase in direct propor-tion to the addition of females to the sexual mix.

To the purist, this type of sexual activity might not be regarded as expense account oriented, since it lacks the ele-ment of *quid pro quo*. But who's paying the hotel bill, the bar bill, and the dinner check? Not the participants. It's all on the old expense account.

There are business dinners that feature strippers. These are charged to expenses and, realistically, do as much for the education of the businessman as the itinerant economist or the lecture-circuit spokesman for the Free Enterprise System.

I know of a business organization whose annual dinner features a succession of four strippers, each of whom takes off just a little bit more, until the last is down to the buff. Another group rents a riverboat and stocks it with food and booze, topless waitresses, and a string of strippers heavily into audience participation.

These affairs are justified as business expenses because, between the acts, much of the conversation is business or-iented. Things like, "I wonder how much she would charge for a blow job?"

Procuring sex partners in a business situation is a delicate task and is handled with the utmost discretion. There are code words to be learned and great care to be taken to avoid embarrassing or offending. In Taiwan, suggesting a "hot lunch" has nothing to do with the temperature of the food or the amount of chili sauce. It is the Taiwanese equivalent of the Japanese "arrangement." In this country, the seeker-of-favors might talk about "feminine companionship" or cloak his evil intentions in some other innocent-sounding euphe-mism. Everybody likes sex, but some people react negatively if asked directly if they would like to get laid.

A friend in the finance business, who lends money to people nobody else would go near, tells of a fishing trip arranged by a client who was greatly indebted to his financier:

> When he invited me he asked if I had any objection to a little feminine companionship. I said no, but didn't know just what he meant.
>
> Well, the boat was a chartered thirty-footer with a complete bar, a buffet, and two lovely young ladies in attendance. They served drinks and food, and when I sat in my chair and grabbed my fishing pole, one of the young ladies sat on my lap and began fondling me strategically. Soon we each had a pole in hand. I didn't catch a single fish, but it was a delightful day.

He now knows that when feminine companionship is brought up, they're not talking about my Aunt Sadie.

Probably the ultimate in expense account sex is the executive orgy. This is an elaborate affair arranged for top management people only. If properly done, it costs thousands of dollars—roughly the cost of a bar mitzvah or catered wedding. Involved will be a suite of rooms at a top hotel, drinks, dinner, wines, champagne, and, of course, girls. They must be young, beautiful, intelligent, and very good at what they do.

There is no limit to the ingenuity that goes into providing entertainment to suit a customer's proclivities. For instance, what would appear more innocent on a corporate expense record than two airline tickets to Milan, the site of an international trade show, purchased in the names of a corporate officer and his wife? Looks perfectly legitimate. But the corporate officer never used the tickets. Instead, a good customer, who liked international travel and young women, was given the tickets and an attractive, paid companion, who posed as the customer's wife. All expenses, of course, were picked up by the host corporation, and who was any the wiser?

Modeling charges may also be a euphemism for the expense of satisfying an important customer's sexual desires. The girls may very well be models, but the real reason for using that word is that modeling fees and the cost of a first class prostitute are in the same ball park. A manufacturer could not get away with $150-an-hour charges for secretarial services, but that kind of modeling fee would not be questioned.

Another popular form of "entertainment" is known in the trade as "smorgasbord." This is not at the same level as the executive orgy and is generally reserved for conventions where a bunch of the boys get together—a group of buyers being entertained by a supplier or an accountant entertaining a group of clients or prospective clients.

There are drinks all around for an hour or two, then dinner at a fine restaurant with wine and/or more drinks, after-dinner brandy, lots of raucous talk and loud laughter; and, finally, the evening is climaxed when the host asks: "Who wants to get laid?"

All hands go up, and the party moves to a suite of rooms at one of the better hotels in town. By pre-arrangement, the host has the room staffed with party girls (assorted racially and in physical proportions), sometimes naked or topless or elaborately but suggestively gowned. There are more drinks, and soon the girls and the boys are mingling and there is a wide variety of action available: plain sex, kinky sex, simple blow jobs, trips around the world—whatever suits the fancy of the conventioneers; a veritable smorgasbord of sexual delights.

How can this kind of expense be charged to corporate accounts? You can be sure it won't go down as the cost of getting customers laid. One old-time sales representative, experienced in producing these little parties for his customers, would make out an expense report, put in the names of those entertained, the name of the hotel and the cost, and label the event "COCKTAIL party." By writing "cocktail" in capital letters, the boss knew what was meant, but as far as the boys down at the IRS knew, the charge was for a party where food and drink was served and business discussed immediately prior, after, or during the affair.

A rung below the smorgasbord is gangbang, another ritual

that seems to grow out of the hilarity and good fellowship of a business convention. (It happens at legionnaires' conventions too, but these don't count since the jerks are using their own money.) This is a tawdry business in which someone invites to the hotel room a hooker who is prepared to take on any and all comers. This has no class whatsoever, and I'm not sure it belongs in a book on the joys of expense account living.

One of the hazards of the gangbang is the ever-present possibility of contracting a social disease and bringing it home to your wife. This became more than a possibility for a conventioneer I heard about who came home with what is indelicately known as a "dose." Feeling a responsibility to advise a friend who had also participated, he called and broke the grim news. The friend, also a responsible type, felt compelled to tell his wife the whole sordid story and suggested that they both undergo physical examinations. The tests showed neither had the disease.

Conventions and trade shows provide convenient forums for spreading good will through sexual stimulation. Exhibitors who seek to attract attention from potential buyers often use scantily clad women as demonstrators and salespersons. Some of these girls are prepared to moonlight if the customer's orders are big enough.

A friend of mine recently told me of an exhibitor who rented a connecting-room next to his sales exhibit where any customer who wrote an order of five figures or more could go for a quick visit with an employee skilled in the art of fellatio. At a food show, an exhibitor entreated a customer to take his showroom girl up to bed. "She's paid for; so why not use her," he said.

While conventions, with all the drinking and carrying on, tend to lead to sexual encounters, the one-on-one situation is much more delicate. If a seller would like to repay a buyer for past kindnesses or future orders with sexual currency, much care is required. A misreading of the buyer's inclinations

EXPENSE ACCOUNT SEX 59

could be catastrophic. The guy could turn out to be the Pope's cousin, and you could end up losing your firm's best customer.

Techniques vary, but an old Seventh Avenue character who is a full-time salesman and part-time procurer explains it this way:

> I start by feeling the guy out. Maybe a couple of friendly lunches, a dinner, theater tickets, ballgames—the usual thing. If he makes the first move and lets me know he'd like to screw around, it's easy. I set it up and that's it.
>
> But if the buyer plays it straight and spends a lot of time talking about his wife and kids and his work with church socials, it's tough to tell if he's putting on a show or is really an Eagle Scout.
>
> After a couple of social meetings, I'll take him to dinner at a restaurant that has particularly pulchritudinous waitresses or a place that normally swarms with high class hookers. Somewhere during the meal I'll point to an outstanding beauty and say, "Hey, look at that gorgeous hunk over there. I'd love to climb into her."
>
> If my friend is not into that kind of action, he'll either ignore my remark or say something self-righteous, and I'll drop the whole subject like a hot potato. Either this guy is for real or he's queer or he's into cash. In any case, there is no point in pursuing the sex angle.
>
> But if he says something like, "Yeh, so would I," then you go to the next question: "Would you like to get laid?"
>
> The rest is a snap. If he says no, you drop the subject. If he says yes, you've got him. It's not easy for a customer to turn you down when you're giving him that kind of service. Next to putting a guy on your payroll or kicking back a percentage of everything he buys, getting him laid is the best insurance that you're going to get your share, or better, of his business.

Some expense account sex-swingers make it a point to go along with a customer and to join in the festivities. This creates a bond between the two, something like having served in combat together. It also helps to put the customer a bit more at ease, since whatever you've got on him, he's got on you.

Which brings us again to the point of discretion and confidentiality. No salesman wants the whole neighborhood to know he pimps on the side, and buyers are not too fond of having their sexual proclivities bandied about the market. Writing things down is the ultimate sin.

Here is an illustration: A supersalesman is shopping around for an attractive young lady to service some of his better customers, and after a few discreet inquiries he is directed to meet an applicant at a downtown bar. The salesman recalls, "The girl has it all, lovely face, a soft cultured voice, a terrific figure, a beautiful set of twins. My customers would flip. She takes out a book and shows me a list of names of the people she's worked for. All of my competitors. I politely give her a twenty-dollar bill and tell her to take a cab as far as the twenty would take her. The last thing I need is to see *my* name on that goddamn list."

In the face of the sexual revolution, rather than resort to the lay-for-pay girls, some business people prefer a more sporting approach. That is, they supply the date—a secretary, a model, or whatever—and leave it up to the beneficiaries to score or strike out.

It is reported by reliable sources that a certain fur manufacturer maintains a swank East Side apartment which he has placed at the disposal of a handful of perky flight attendants. They come and use the apartment as they please. All the furrier asks is that if he has an important buyer in from out of town, who would like a dinner companion or someone to go dancing with, the girls put forth their best efforts to oblige. They are on their own as to how far they want to go with any of the obligatory dates. If something works out, terrific. If not, there's dinner and a show and goodnight and thanks.

What about women in business? Aren't they entitled to the same treatment as men? Shouldn't they have their sexual pleasures on expense accounts? They certainly are entitled, but whether it's prevalent or not, I can't say. Sure, I've heard lots of stories about "walkers" supplied for women buyers in town, and about stud services for women with influential corporate positions. But this is not the kind of question you can ask a stranger and expect to get answered honestly. Since my sources are people (mostly men) who know me and trust me, I feel on reasonably solid ground when talking about men and expense account sex. I'll leave the feminine side of the story to the researchers, such as Masters and Johnson, who are naive enough to think that if you ask enough strangers very personal questions you'll come up with a realistic conclusion.

Now to the matter of why sex is used as a selling tool. Ours is a competitive economy in which the market sets prices, and the business that fails to keep up with the competition folds. If there are a large number of suppliers available with the same merchandise at the same price, why would a buyer pick one over the other? Service, reliability, personal relationships, family, locality, local pride, convenience, inertia . . . there are many reasons, and sex fits in somewhere.

One salesman put it simply: "Say there are four of us after the same order. Our products are pretty much the same, and so are our prices. But I'm getting the buyer laid. Who do you think will get his business?"

, A collection agency, which has since gone into bankruptcy, used sex as a selling tool and a visual aid. A sexy-voiced lady would call a prospective client on the phone and go into a routine explaining what a fine job her company did in collecting delinquent accounts. She would request that claims be turned over to her; then she would bring out the big gun: "Rather than mailing your claims in, why not bring them down to Miami Beach personally? We'll rent a hotel room for you, and I'll be your hostess for the weekend."

Another approach by this company was to send a salesman, accompanied by a decorative young lady, to visit prospects in person. The salesman would make his pitch while the girl just sat in the chair smiling and uncrossing her legs and generally doing her best to tacitly demonstrate that she was part of the package.

The company apparently couldn't afford the expensive sales force because when it was successful in obtaining claims for collection it neglected to turn the money collected over to its clients.

The attitude of some businessmen in management positions is one of live and let live. "If my sales people are getting buyers laid, I don't want to know about it," one high level manager told me. "As long as they're bringing in business, I don't question their expense accounts. If the expense slips for five taxi rides and two lunches [under twenty-five dollars so they don't have to be documented] are really to cover the cost of getting a client laid, that's not my concern. My job is to see that they produce. If they do a good job, there will be no problems with expense accounts."

Lest it be inferred that corporate sex is pretty much confined to the garment business, where cash sales provide ready financing, remember the multi-million dollar slush funds that large international corporations were able to accumulate for foreign bribes and political contributions. You can be damned sure that these corporate giants have little trouble finding funds to get their clients appropriate bed partners.

While it was suggested that I research this portion of the book by personally participating, I relied, instead, on interviews with reliable sources. The closest I ever came to expense account sex was at one of New York's better night clubs, some years ago. While watching the show from the bar, I was approached by a lovely young lady who was the embodiment of all my sexual fantasies—dark, silky hair flowing all the way down to the sensual curve at the base of her back, a smile just this side of Farrah Fawcett Majors, and a gown of the sheerest lavender gossamer.

She began to make small talk about the show and New York City and her hometown in Ohio, and I was all aglow with the thought that I was so irresistible that this dream picked me out of a bar full of single men. She asked me what I did for a living, and I lied about being a famous writer, and then I asked what she did.

"I'm a private entertainer," she said.

"What's a private entertainer?"

"I entertain your privates."

My host for the evening, an executive with a reputation as a big expense account liver, said he was prepared to finance some private entertainment, "up to fifty bucks," but this lady was out of his price range. I had another drink and went home.

CHAPTER SEVEN

Documentation

The Paper Chase

WHEN YOU ENTER the world of expense account living you will deal with at least two bureaucracies: your own company and the IRS.

Regardless of the stated purpose of any bureaucracy, its real reason for being is to generate paper. So if you want to be successful and come out a winner in the expense account, perks game, you must be prepared to document. You'll need receipts, expense reports, diaries, charge account vouchers, and cancelled checks. This is the stuff from which expense account living draws sustenance—and can be a real pain. But saving paper sure beats the hell out of spending your own money.

Although the documentation provided by receipts, cancelled checks, invoices and the like is best, a diary maintained contemporaneously with the expenditures can be of great help if the IRS decides to get stuffy about your expenses. It is not unheard of for a diary to be prepared for an entire year's expenses on the night before a scheduled visit with an IRS agent, but this is a fraudulent technique and has no place in this book.

However, it does remind me of a story an accountant friend told me about a rather clumsy effort to fake expenses. The accountant audited one client's travel and entertainment records year after year, and everything seemed in order. There were diary entries with receipts from restaurants stapled to the appropriate pages to document the entries. But the accountant began to get a vague feeling of deja vu.

"Somehow," the accountant recalled, "the receipts looked familiar to me. Then I noticed they had no dates on them and there were extra staple holes in the corners. That was the give-away. The son-of-a-bitch had been using the same receipts, year after year."

For the legitimate diary keeper, the accounting firm of Laventhol and Horwath has published a helpful pamphlet on the entire subject of T&E: *The Internal Revenue Service Takes a Hard Look at Travel and Entertainment Expenses*, February 1978. The pamphlet describes what a diary entry for a business lunch might have looked like in 1578:

> Up betimes and thence to my office where I became steeped in paperwork and scrivening. Before midday, was visited by young Will Shakespeare who entreated me to sponsor publickly some doggeral he had written pertaining to dreams in midsummer— an effort of little avail. As a kindly gesture, escorted Will to the Boar's Head Publick House where we feasted sumptuously on roasted mutton, laced with strong ale. Will recited many passages from his new writings, including an impressive metaphor between the lives of mortals and players upon the stage. Was persuaded to examine all MSS at my leisure. The repast cost a pound, 2 shillings and ha'pence, and the innkeeper will provide me with a written accounting for my records. 'Twill be full value returned if the writings prove fortunate—and methinks they shall. A day of pleasure, an evening of ennui, and so to bed.

This entry has all the essentials: amount spent, where, who was entertained, the date, business purpose, and business relationship. Furthermore, the innkeeper's bill will also be available.

Since today we operate at a much faster pace than the Elizabethan producer, the updated entry would be simply, "lunch, Feb. 1, Boar's Head Inn, Will Shakespeare, playwrite; plugging new play; may click at the box office; 10 pounds, 50 pence." The updated price is not expense account padding, but merely the result of the rising cost of mutton and strong ale over the centuries.

There's an old story about actor John Barrymore being sent on a publicity tour and being asked by his studio to be sure to keep a record of his expenses, which the studio agreed to pay. Barrymore, who had no patience with details, submitted the following record:

Cigars for trip to airport	$3.00
Miscellaneous	$5,000.00
Total Cost of the trip	$5,003.00

In those days of low tax rates and free-spending Hollywood studios, a big star could get away with that kind of record keeping. But today, the IRS expects a little more specificity.

There was a time when the IRS and taxpayers would go through a negotiating process under what was known as the "Cohan rule." This resulted from a decision involving entertainer George M. Cohan, who was allowed to deduct a reasonable amount for expenses, based on his extensive business travel and lifestyle, although he kept no records of any consequence. Mr. Cohan had the same lack of respect for paperwork as Barrymore.

Under the Cohan rule the revenue agents and taxpayers would bargain with each other until there was an agreement to allow a certain percentage of the deductions, forty percent, fifty percent, or whatever. Once a taxpayer had established a level of expenses allowed under a Cohan rule arrangement, he would raise it year after year. The system may have saved some auditing time for the agents, but it also resulted in a lot of unsubstantiated and probably unjustified expenses. These days, either you have the documentation, or you're out of luck; that is, unless you maintain a diary and keep individual expense items below twenty-five dollars.

An irate accountant complained to me about his problems with some of his sleazier clients. "Some of these guys are such crooks they'll skim off $200 a week in cash with under twenty-five dollar charges, but they're too lazy to enter anything in a diary. Then they expect me to clear them through the IRS. They have plenty of time to steal, but they don't have the time to make the diary entries."

A booklet prepared by Arthur Young and Company in 1978 on record-keeping requirements for travel, entertainment, and business gift expenditures cautions that the IRS does not allow deductions for "approximations or estimates of expenditures." A diary or account book should be supported by documentary evidence. Entries should be made as close to the actual time of the expenditure as possible, since tax regulations note that a "timely" recording of expenses has more credibility than statements prepared long after the fact.

The booklet adds, however, that it's not necessary to record every single expenditure. The daily cost of meals while traveling can be lumped together, and incidental items like cab fares and phone calls may also be totaled on a daily basis. Receipts or bills are required for lodging expenses incurred while traveling away from home and for any expenditure of twenty-five dollars or more.

If you do not have documentation for travel or entertainment expenses, the IRS may take your word if you can corroborate the expenses with statements from other persons involved in the activity or from someone who received a business gift. The accounting firm booklet notes, however, that the corroborative evidence is tough to get, and the IRS is not required to accept it.

If your boss gives you a per diem allowance for travel and meals, there is no need to make an itemized accounting if the allowance falls within the federal guidelines for various locations. Generally the maximum allowance is forty-four dollars a day (this was 1978, remember). But for New York City, the rate is fifty dollars a day (a rate which, I have heard, IRS agents visiting New York for audits found unrealistically low for their own living expenses) and in Prudhoe Bay, Alaska, one-hundred and forty dollars. Incidentally, Arthur Young points out, the per diem rule does not apply to relatives of the employer. A relative has to make an itemized accounting of expenditures.

The booklet also warns of a requirement to report as income any per diem allowance received in excess of the amount actually spent. It does not, however, indicate how many taxpayers take advantage of this wonderful opportunity to increase their tax payments to Uncle Sam. How many of us remember making deliveries on foot as kids, instead of taking buses or cabs, and then pocketing the fare? And how many reported it on their income taxes?

The New York State Society of Certified Public Accountants estimates that thousands of taxpayers lose millions of dollars in legitimate business expenses because of the lack of documentation. The CPAs cite the case of a Texas doctor who was successful in deducting thousands of dollars spent on a luxurious yacht. (This occurred prior to the 1978 tax law, and while yachts may no longer be deductible, the illustration of the importance of detailed records remains valid.) The doctor contended that he used the yacht exclusively for the entertainment of other doctors who referred patients to him. He maintained a ship's log with the names of the guests, the dates they were aboard, a record of the cases referred to him by each guest, and bills, receipts, or cancelled checks covering all costs of operating the yacht.

In the case of another Texan, this one a Dallas lawyer, the

absence of complete records cost him nearly $6,000 in lost deductions. It seems the lawyer entertained clients and business associates just about every business day at an exclusive luncheon club. He retained the bills for each meal, which showed the date and the amount spent. However, he neglected to note the names of the people entertained or the business purpose of the meals. A tax court ruling held the records inadequate, and the lawyer lost the deductions.

This same lawyer lost another tax case in which one of the essentials was missing. He spent $3,900 on a birthday party for himself, at which about half the guests were clients and another twenty percent, law partners. Although the party promoted good will, the tax court disallowed the deduction because the party was not preceded nor followed by any "substantial business discussion." Just what is meant by "substantial" in this context is difficult to determine, but if you want to satisfy the IRS, there must at least be some business discussion reported.

In dealing with your own company, it also pays to use great care in documenting expenses. Even if the company doesn't require receipts on expenses of less than twenty-five dollars, it won't hurt to submit receipts when they are readily obtainable. I'm not saying that you should clutter up your expense reports with fifty cent toll receipts or two dollar cab fares, but if you have a fifteen dollar lunch or spend twelve dollars for drinks, receipts will add a comfort factor to your company's accounting department. Your company must deal with the IRS, and since the government is document-happy, detailed records and supporting documents will certainly be helpful.

One simple tip at the outset—accounting departments pride themselves on accuracy, so be sure all the numbers on your expense sheet add up. You will find that more expense slips are bounced back to their authors simply because of faulty addition or subtraction than for any other reason. And once an expense slip is separated from the flow of paper, it automatically becomes the subject of extra scrutiny.

Incidentally, the use of the word "authors" in referring to expense account writers was no accident. Technically, an expense account is an objective tabulation of facts and figures; but in the real world, objectivity is an illusive concept, and we must recognize that man's (and woman's) creative instincts cannot be completely suppressed.

CHAPTER EIGHT

Inside the IRS

The War between Men and Machines

THE FEDERAL TAX SYSTEM, which makes the government an equal partner in everything you earn after you reach a modicum of success, is the driving force behind the push for expense account money and tax-exempt perks.

A single taxpayer in 1978, whose taxable income topped $32,000 a year, moved into the fifty percent bracket. For a married couple filing jointly, the fifty percent bracket arrived at the $44,000 level. Income above that will be taxed as high as seventy percent, but there is a provision limiting the total tax on earned income to fifty percent; so those in the upper salary brackets will not have to turn over more than half of their salaries to the federal government.

With that kind of tax bite, tax-free money becomes a kind of supermoney. Every one dollar in expense account money is worth as much as two dollars in earned income. Thus, the incentive is created to try to get the more valuable money. In a sense, it's a reversal of Gresham's Law. Old Gresham said that bad money will tend to drive good money out of circulation. What happens in high-tax countries is that tax-free money (good money) tends to drive taxable money (bad money) out of circulation. Whatever you can get with expense account money will be that much cheaper than it would be using taxable money. Furthermore, since corporations generally have more spare money around than individuals, it's reasonable that business is the place to look for your spending money.

The higher the tax rate, the more profitable and tempting it becomes to channel income and expenditures into the tax-exempt category. Unfortunately, it's not always legal. In Sweden, for example, where a pervasive welfare state has pushed tax rates to confiscatory levels, a barter system has developed: a carpenter might build a cabinet for a dentist in exchange for an upper plate. Since no money is involved, no income is reported.

High taxes in Sweden have virtually eliminated the possibility to accumulate wealth from salary alone (no Swede's take home pay can ever be more than three-and-a-half times the after-tax salary of any other Swede) and such luxuries as yachts and expensive summer homes might be expected to disappear. They haven't, and a good part of the money for such amenities comes from business expenses and executive perks.

The Swiss, who have a worldwide reputation for honesty and integrity in financial matters, are nevertheless no strangers to expense account padding. It is customary in Switzerland for waiters to leave dates blank on restaurant checks so those with expense accounts can fill in whatever date suits their particular needs.

A study of tax rates by the Conference Board, a business-oriented research organization, found that among the major industrial nations taxes are highest in Denmark, Sweden, and the United Kingdom. "I have friends in England who never eat in a restaurant unless it's on an expense account," a United States executive told me. "And these are not people that I would classify as poverty-level. The tax rates there are so confiscatory that people are virtually forced to look to expense account money for a few luxuries."

The Conference Board study, based on 1975 figures, found that personal income taxes came to twenty-eight percent of household income in Denmark, twenty-three percent in Sweden, sixteen percent in the United Kingdom, and fourteen percent in Canada. The United States ranked tenth in this category at eleven percent. It should be stressed that these are the rates paid on total income and cover all income levels— from the bottom to the top. At the low end of the tax spectrum were Italy and France (two countries where tax evasion ranks as a national sport with soccer and automobile racing), with effective tax rates of five percent.

With United States households paying an average of eleven percent of income for federal taxes (this does not include an additional eight percent for social security payments), it is clear that there is quite a gap between nominal rates and real rates, thanks to armies of accountants, tax advisors, and other experts who help taxpayers avoid, if not evade, taxes.

In its efforts to minimize tax evasion and avoidance, the IRS has a large audit division, which in recent years has been reinforced by a number of computer programs that help select returns that look most promising from the point of view of producing additional revenue for the government. The IRS tries to be cost-effective and is not interested in spending time auditing returns and coming up dry. However, despite all the sophisticated systems, one out of every four returns audited remains unchanged. But those that are changed produce considerable revenue.

In 1977, auditing efforts resulted in additional income tax and penalty assessments of $1,982,748,000 against corporations and $1,407,760,000 against individual taxpayers. That year, the IRS received 85,611,000 individual income tax returns and audited a total of 1,892,786. During the same year, it received 2,247,000 corporate income tax returns and audited 167,689.

Therefore, the chances against an individual's return being audited were about forty-five to one; corporation's faced tougher odds, about thirteen to one.

The formula used in programming the computers to pick out likely audit candidates is top secret and is revealed only on a "need to know" basis. IRS officials concluded that readers of this book do not qualify. Nevertheless, there is no doubt that since a major criterion is the likelihood of recovering additional taxes, the computer will look for large incomes and out-of-line deductions. As Jerry Davis, audit manager for the IRS in Washington, put it, "We have to measure the cost against the degree of compliance."

In addition to selecting returns, the IRS computers verify the mathematics on returns and the IRS is fast developing a program of matching returns with information, received from other computers, on payments of wages, interest, and dividends.

There has been an explosive growth in recent years in the number of organizations reporting and the amount of information being received on magnetic tape. In 1966, the IRS received some 26,248,000 documents to tape from 591 reporting entities. By 1977 this computer information flow had surged to 245,277,000 documents from 35,330 separate reporting organizations. With this increase in available information, the IRS, in 1975, began matching these data with tax returns to try to spot nonfilers or unreported income. Bad news for tax evaders.

All returns are checked manually on receipt to pick up incomplete forms and errors, such as duplication or failure to follow instructions. A computer then monitors the mathematics.

There are two computer-based systems for selecting returns to be audited. The primary method is a computer program of mathematical formulas called the Discriminant Function System (DIF), which identifies returns having the highest potential for error. As a result of this program, the IRS says, audits resulting in no tax changes have been reduced from forty-three percent in 1968 to twenty-four percent in 1977. The formulas are constantly being revised and refined. A new one was installed for individual and partnership returns filed in 1978.

Returns are also chosen for audit under a computerized system that makes a random selection within income classes for research and statistical purposes. These audits serve to provide taxpayer reporting characteristics used to keep the DIF formulas up-to-date. Audits of this type are generally quite intensive because of the desire to generate a great deal of information.

The computer selection gets some help from manual operations which screen incomes above certain levels. Some taxpayers applying for refunds after their tax returns are filed are also subject to human scrutiny.

Although the tax people collect substantial sums through audit procedures, criminal prosecutions are relatively rare. In 1977 there were a total of 2,695 federal tax cases referred for prosecution, of which 1,636 actually resulted in indictments or criminal informations. When you compare these figures with the total number of returns filed in that year (133,685,000), you can reach two conclusions. One is that the overwhelming number of taxpayers are honest. The other is that there are a lot of people out there getting away with murder. I agree with both conclusions.

If you find yourself in disagreement with the IRS on what you should or should not pay, there are a number of avenues of appeal open. First, you can argue with the agent doing the audit and try to convince him or her that you don't owe the money.

An accountant with much experience dealing with IRS agents told me about a novel argument he used. The agent came in for an audit on one of the accountant's best clients, a company that earned about $1,000,000 in the year in question and paid $500,000 in taxes. After spending three days going over the records, the agent found that everything was properly documented and accounted for except $3,000, which the IRS man wanted to disallow.

The accountant thought the agent was being unfair. "Suppose you were a partner in a business but did no work for it," the accountant told the agent. "Now suppose every year your partner sent you $500,000 as your share. Then you discover that there was about $1,500 that might still be owing to you. Would you break up the partnership over that?" The agent thought the story was amusing and smiled with sympathy and understanding. He disallowed the $3,000 in unsubstantiated deductions.

If you strike out with the agent, you can go to a supervisor or group manager to make your pitch. IRS audit program manager Davis, who worked his way up from trainee through the ranks of agent and group manager, told me that generally the group manager will back the agent, but "there have been occasions when I, as a group manager, overturned an agent's decision after hearing the taxpayer's story."

Once the informal argument route is exhausted, there is a formal framework within the agency. There had been a two-level appeals system with a district conference and a higher, regional tribunal. But in 1978, the IRS decided that the system was redundant and expensive. The district appeal was eliminated, and beginning October 2, 1978, all appeals were routed directly to one of seven regional offices.

If the dispute cannot be resolved within the agency, the taxpayer can then appeal to the United States Tax Court. A simplified procedure exists, somewhat like small claims court, for disputes involving $1,500 or less in any one tax year. Arguing under the small claims procedure does not require the knowledge of legal process needed in a full scale court case; so the taxpayer need not hire expensive legal help. There is one drawback to the small claims procedure. If you lose the case, that's final. There is no further appeal. Other tax court decisions may be appealed through the federal court system— first to the United States Court of Appeals and then up to the United States Supreme Court. It is also possible to by-pass the tax court and take the case directly to the federal district court.

From there it can go up to the United States Court of Appeals and then to the Supreme Court.

Of course all this appealing will cost a bundle; so before going ahead with an all-out fight with the IRS, consider the alternatives. You might be much better off to pay the money and then hope the odds work out better for you in the years ahead. After all, how often does a forty-five to one shot come in.

What happens if the government disallows a T&E deduction and all appeal routes are exhausted or you decide against appealing? You have to pay the tax, plus interest. The interest rate is reviewed every November, but in 1979, it was six percent, a modest figure indeed.

If a corporation as well as an individual is involved, the disallowance will result in double tax. First the corporation will have to pay taxes on the expenditure since it cannot be included as a business expense (lower expenses mean higher profits, hence higher taxes). The individual who benefited from the payment is charged with the extra income and he must pay tax on that too.

If the company had paid the extra money as regular compensation, that would have been a deductible business expense and the individual would have had to pay tax on it at his regular rate. The net effect, then, of a deduction that is disallowed is the creation of nonexistent, but taxable, profits.

If there is a finding of willful intent to evade taxes, there is a penalty of fifty percent of the tax due and the possibility of criminal proceedings. However, most fraud cases are closed without criminal action. An IRS spokesman said that there are about 7,000 fraudulent cases a year and only 1,500 to 1,600 criminal prosecutions.

CHAPTER NINE

Taxes and T&E

Breaking the Language Barrier

THERE IS LITTLE CORRELATION between the language of the tax experts and English. Anyone who has ever had to plow through a tax form and its instructions is well aware of this. So before going ahead with the rules of deducting T&E expenses, I think we should try to overcome the language barrier.

The IRS distinguishes between travel and transportation; foreign travel is not the same as travel "outside the United States; business meals are different from business entertainment"; and, as a famous professional once said, "a house is not a home."

Travel is better than transportation, for tax purposes, because, when you're on travel status, you can deduct all sorts of expenses that go beyond mere transportation.

Foreign travel covers anything beyond the United States, its territories, and possessions, while travel outside the United

States includes any trip outside the fifty states. This becomes significant in deductions for conventions because there are much tougher standards for deducting expenses of foreign conventions than for domestic conventions. A meeting in the Virgin Islands would not be classified as a foreign convention. A convention in Bermuda would be foreign.

The requirements for deducting business meals are less stringent than those for other forms of business entertainment.

And, finally, your idea of your home and the tax man's idea of your home can be miles apart.

The IRS official publication, *Travel, Entertainment and Gift Expenses,* says that travel expenses "are the ordinary and necessary expenses incurred in traveling away from home in pursuit of your business, profession, or employment. These expenses may be deducted if you substantiate them. . . . However, you may not deduct such expenses to the extent they are lavish or extravagant under the circumstances or were incurred for personal vacation purposes." Then it goes on to warn the taxpayer not to confuse travel expenses with transportation, which is explained in another section.

"Transportation expenses include the cost of travel by air, rail, bus, taxi, etc., and the cost of operating and maintaining your automobile, but *not* (IRS italics) the cost of meals and lodging. Transportation expenses directly attributable to the actual conduct of your business or employment may be deducted . . . even if you were not away from home."

If you're confused, don't worry. So was I until I looked into the matter further. It appears that the principal difference between travel and transportation expenses is that you can't have travel expenses unless you are away from home, but you can have transportation expenses.

If you take a cab to visit a customer during the day, the money you spend for the cab is deductible as a transportation expense. Maybe you could have taken a bus and saved yourself and the government some money, but the IRS doesn't get involved at that level unless it can show that the expense "was lavish or extravagant under the circumstances," or am I confusing transportation with travel?

The cost of commuting to or from your job is not deductible and the IRS makes that perfectly clear. "Commuting expenses are nondeductible notwithstanding the distance between your home and your regular place of work or if you are employed at different locations on different days within the same city or general area." In other words, if you want to live in Philadelphia and work in New York, that's your problem. The government is not prepared to subsidize such foolishness. Even if you carry a bunch of work-related tools to or from your job in your car, it doesn't help. The trip is not deductible. But if you have to rent a trailer to carry the extra equipment, then the additional cost of the trailer is deductible.

If you want to deduct "travel" expenses as opposed to "transportation" costs, you have to be on travel status. How does one get on travel status? It's not easy and there are an assortment of exceptions, but basically it's this. You have to be away from home overnight or at least long enough to require sleeping accommodations.

The IRS says you don't have to be away for a full twenty-four hour period, just so long as it's "substantially longer than an ordinary day's work and, during released time while away, it is reasonable to get sleep or rest to meet the demands of your employment or business." A quick nap in your car will not be enough to put you on "travel" status. But once you get such status, you can deduct a bunch of stuff:

- All transportation costs between cities and within, plus baggage charges and costs of moving around any illustrative material.
- Meals, lodging, cleaning and laundry expenses.
- Telephone, telegraph, public stenographer's fees.
- Operation and maintenance of house trailers.
- Tips incidental to any of these expenses.
- Other similar expenses incidental to being away from home.

How far away do you have to go to be away from home? At one time if you traveled twenty miles you might be considered "away from home" for tax purposes. But that's been changed. As far as the IRS is concerned, your home is your place of business (even if you live in Philadelphia and work in New York). If you don't have a regular place of business, for one reason or another, then your home is where you live. Finally, if you don't have a regular place of business and you don't have a real residence, then you're considered an "itinerant," and wherever you happen to hang your hat at any time is your home. An itinerant can never be on travel status and deduct expenses because, since he has no home, he can never be away from it.

Assuming there's no problem determining your home (for tax purposes, that is), if business takes you out of the "entire city" or "general area of your tax home" for long enough to need some rest—substantial rest, not just a catnap—you're on travel status and can deduct the cost of having your shirts laundered. (I know some people who take all their dirty clothes with them when they go on a trip so they can have them laundered for free by their companies. This is not what the IRS had in mind.)

The IRS test, which uses length of time away from home to determine travel status, creates a problem at the other end of the spectrum. How long do you have to be away from home to establish a new home? There is no end to the complications of determining what you and I regard as a simple matter. Where is your home, or, as the government puts it, your tax home?

For instance (this is an example given by the IRS), you live in Pittsburgh where you work twelve weeks a year. But for the rest of the time you work in Baltimore for the same employer. While in Baltimore you eat out and stay at a rooming house. You may think you live in Pittsburgh, but the IRS says you live in Baltimore because that's where you work most of the year. When you're in Baltimore, you cannot deduct meals and lodging and all the other items allowed to one on travel status. But while you're in Pittsburgh, living where you think is home, you can deduct "that portion of your family living expenses for meals and lodging properly attributable to your presence in Pittsburgh while working there."

Now, if you work for a company in Cincinnati and are assigned to another location, say Pittsburgh, where you thought you lived before, when does your tax home become Pittsburgh? A "temporary assignment" to Pittsburgh would not change your tax home. It will remain Cincinnati, and you could deduct your meals and laundry while in Pittsburgh. The government defines a temporary assignment as one for a fixed and reasonably short period. Any assignment expected to last a year or more will generally not be considered temporary. Also, if an assignment is "indefinite," which means "its termination cannot be foreseen within a fixed and reasonably short period," then your tax home becomes Pittsburgh, and you have to start paying your own laundry bills.

Moreover, the IRS says, if your employer thinks you're away from home (but the IRS does not) and gives you a special allowance for living expenses, which you account for, that money has to be included in your income and will be taxed. With an attitude like that, it's easy to understand why the IRS never makes the list of all-time favorite government agencies.

IRS agents are a suspicious lot. There was this manufacturer with a condominium in Florida, a business in New York, and a large New York apartment. Since the New York apartment was by far the more elaborate and costly of his two residences, he tried to deduct its cost from his income. He contended that he lived in Florida and kept the New York apartment for the convenience of his business and for business entertaining. Generally he spent four or five days a week in New York.

The suspicious agent was convinced he was being hustled. The agent concluded that the man actually lived in New York and the Florida apartment was a place to go to get away from the cold weather. The agent disallowed deductions for the

New York apartment, except for substantiated business entertainment. As to the Florida apartment, there could be no business use for that. The manufacturer didn't do any business in Florida.

Now to entertainment expenses. These, the IRS says, are not included in travel expenses. If you want to deduct entertainment expenses, you have to look at another complete set of rules. Forget about whether you're away from home or even if you have a home. Entertainment expenses are another breed of cat.

For entertainment expenses to be deductible they must be either "directly related" or "associated with" the active conduct of your business, or covered under one of the exceptions. The business meal is one of the exceptions.

Business meals qualify for deductions if they are furnished "under circumstances generally considered conducive to a business discussion." You need not actually have a business discussion, just as long as the person or persons you are treating to lunch or dinner or drinks have the kind of relationship to you that makes business sense. A night club where the entertainment might intrude on a business discussion, if one were to develop, "is not considered a suitable environment," the IRS says.

Generally business meals are taken in restaurants or hotel dining rooms, but food and drinks served at home may also qualify if the principal purpose was to benefit business and not primarily social.

In fact, you don't even have to show up at a business meal for it to be deductible. For instance, a dental equipment supplier can buy a table at an association banquet for dentists who are his customers or potential customers. The equipment supplier could skip the dinner, spend the evening watching television, and still take a deduction. This kind of good will gesture comes within the business meal exception.

What about "lavish or extravagant" meals. The IRS attitude appears to be that it's not its function to dictate where people should have lunch or what they should eat. As long as the business meal is held in an atmosphere conducive to a business discussion and conforms with industry or business custom, the IRS probably won't worry about the size of the tab.

Audit programmer Davis told me that the IRS is preparing guidelines to better define "lavish or extravagant." "There has been very little litigation on the question to provide guidance," he said. "Right now, it's a matter of judgment and industry practice." In the IRS instructions, following the statement that lavish expenditures will not be allowed for deduction, there is this amplification: "Entertainment expenses will not be disallowed merely because they exceed a fixed dollar amount or are incurred at deluxe restaurants, hotels, night clubs, and resort establishments. An expense will not be considered lavish or extravagant if it is reasonable considering the facts and circumstances."

The question of lavish or extravagant is not even discussed in connection with business meals, only in the general area of business entertainment.

To classify a business expense as "directly related" entertainment, you must show "you had more than a general expectation of deriving income or some other specific benefit at some future time," you actually engaged in business during the entertainment period, or the main purpose of the occasion was to transact business. You are not required to show that the money spent for "directly related" entertainment actually resulted in income or some other business benefit. The IRS permits you to throw some of your (and their) money down the tubes, as long as your intentions are honorable.

Also covered under "directly related" expenses are those "occurring in a clear business setting," for instance, entertainment in the hospitality room at a convention. Entertainment that has the effect of returning some of the money received from customers is another type of expenditure considered in this category. The IRS calls this a "price rebate" and mentions, as an example, occasional free meals given by a restaurant owner to good customers.

Finally, the IRS says, it is possible to entertain people with whom you have no business relationship and deduct the expenses as "directly related" if the occasion would help publicize your business. As an example, the IRS cites entertainment of civic or business leaders to publicize the opening of a hotel or a new show.

One of the splashiest promotions of the past decade, that might fit this last category, was a week-long cruise in 1973 paid for by an oil magnate to celebrate the completion of a new $200 million oil refinery in Canada.

At a cost in the neighborhood of $1 million, this oilman chartered the *Queen Elizabeth II* and transported to Canada some 900 VIPs—top executives of other oil companies, politicians, and other dignitaries—plus their spouses. Each couple was given an outside stateroom and enjoyed the entertainment the *Queen Elizabeth II* normally provides on its cruises, plus free meals and free drinks. Even the tips were taken care of by the host. In the port of Halifax, the entire Halifax Symphony Orchestra came aboard to entertain. The only amusement the guests had to pay for themselves was gambling in the ship's casino. There were some heavy losses, but rumor has it that some of the losers were able to convert their bad luck into business costs that slipped into expense vouchers and were reimbursed by the VIPs' respective employers.

One reason the oilman gave for chartering the luxury liner, instead of just flying guests up to the refinery, was that there were no hotels in the area that could hold 1,800 people.

This same big spender chartered the *Queen Elizabeth II* on two other occasions for three-day trips to Bermuda to mark the launching of a new morning paper in New York City. Ironically, the newspaper never got off the ground, and the Canadian refinery soon went bankrupt and was mothballed for years while creditors wrangled over who had the rights to what. As I said earlier, the IRS doesn't expect all entertainment expenses to pay off.

In addition to "directly related" entertainment expenses, the government permits deduction of "associated" entertainment expenses. An entertainment expenditure would be considered associated with the active conduct of business "if the entertainment directly precedes or follows a substantial and bona fide business discussion." Directly preceding or following means on the same day, but the IRS makes allowances for special circumstances and will bend a little.

The Sperry Rand dinner mentioned earlier would probably qualify under "associated" entertainment even though it was held the evening before the business meeting. The IRS says, "If both the entertainment and the business discussion do not occur on the same day, the facts and circumstances in each case will be considered to see if the rule is met. Among the facts to be considered are the place, date, and duration of the business discussion, whether you or your business associates are from out of town, and if so, the dates of arrival and departure, and the reasons the entertainment and discussions did not take place on the same day."

If you spend money for entertainment associated with your business but some of the guests are unrelated to the business purposes, you can't deduct the money spent on them. However, wives and husbands get special treatment.

As the IRS puts it, in impeccable bureaucratese, "Ordinarily, the portion of an entertainment expense, otherwise deductible, allocable to the spouse of a person who engaged in the discussion will be considered associated with the active conduct of your business."

But just when you might think the IRS has gone soft, it plants this zinger: "You may not deduct the cost of entertainment allocable to your spouse or the spouse of a business customer unless you can show that you had a clear business purpose rather than a personal or social purpose in incurring such expense."

Hold on. Does that mean you can't deduct the cost of taking your wife or husband along on an evening of business entertainment? Not at all.

If you entertain a business customer and the customer's spouse joins you "because it is impractical, under the circumstances, to entertain the customer without the spouse," the cost of the spouse is deductible. "Furthermore, if your spouse joins the party because the customer's spouse is present, the cost of the entertainment allocable to your spouse is also considered an ordinary and necessary business expense."

Then again, the government says, "If your spouse accompanies you on a business trip or convention, that portion of the expenses attributable to travel, meals, and lodging for your spouse is not deductible, unless you can prove a bona fide business purpose for your spouse's presence. Incidental services, such as typing notes or assisting in entertaining customers, are not sufficient to warrant a deduction."

Now, if you take your secretary along. . . .

The definition of a substantial business discussion is necessarily vague since one person's substance is another's froth. The IRS says it depends on the circumstances. About the best it can come up with is that you must show that you "actively engaged in a discussion, meeting, negotiation, or other bona fide business transaction, other than entertainment to obtain income or some other specific business benefit."

The IRS says a substantial discussion does not have to last for any specified length of time nor does it have to account for more time than the entertainment portion. Furthermore, there need be no business discussion during the entertainment period.

Entertainment expenditures to create good will are deductible under the exception for business meals and, therefore, are considered to be associated with business if there is a substantial business discussion before or after the entertainment, which must be provided in a clear business setting, such as a convention or trade show. Domestic conventions and trade shows get virtual carte blanche for associated entertainment expenses, as long as they are sponsored by business and professional organizations and their expenses qualify as "ordinary and necessary."

Interviewed at the IRS office in downtown Washington, Davis said that he thought conventions could be extremely good for business but that they were an ever-present potential for abuse. One of the most frequently abused areas, according to Davis, is foreign conventions. "The business reasons for holding a convention overseas are often nonexistent. Why go to Israel to listen to lectures on corporate law? What special expertise would be found there?"

As a result of the propensity to use foreign conventions as an excuse for vacationing overseas, there has been considerable tightening of the requirements for deductions, and more may be on the way. At this writing, there is a bill being kicked around Congress that might further restrict foreign conventions. If passed, this bill would revise the present rules and allow no deductions for conventions held outside of North America unless there were a good business reason for doing so.

There is no limit on the number of domestic conventions that can be charged off as business expenses, but the law now allows only two, tax-deductible foreign conventions a year, per individual. A business can participate in any number of foreign conventions, but an individual employee is limited to two a year. An individual who goes to more than two can select the two he wants to claim as deductions—probably the two most expensive. Reporting requirements for foreign meetings are much stiffer than for the domestic variety.

Foreign conventions refer to meetings held outside the United States, its possessions, and the Trust Territory of the Pacific. This should not be confused with travel outside the United States, which includes anything outside the fifty states. A trip to Puerto Rico would be considered outside the United States, and requirements for deduction of the trip would be somewhat stiffer than for domestic travel, but a convention held there would not be considered a foreign convention.

A trip within the United States that is primarily for pleasure but which may involve a little business is deductible for the amount attributable to the business portion. However, on travel outside the United States, a trip that is primarily a vacation with some incidental business may be completely nondeductible.

The rule on overseas travel appears to be directed at professionals who schedule seminars at exotic places to take tax-deductible foreign vacations. The example given by the IRS is that of a doctor who goes on a two-week trip overseas, sponsored by his professional association. The trip includes six, two-hour professional seminars: "Your participation in some incidental activity related to your trade or business, the six, two-hour professional seminars, did not convert what was essentially a vacation into a business trip. The expenses incurred for travel were not related primarily to your trade or business, and no other expenses were incurred that were directly attributable to the conduct of your trade or business. Therefore, none of the cost of your trip is deductible as an ordinary and necessary business expense."

If the convention were sponsored by a lot of sick people, and attendance by the doctor might help bring him some new patients, then the IRS might look at the trip differently. However, this point is not covered in the publication.

I might also add that it is still possible to get in on tax deductible vacations through conventions. There's a real estate operator who has a simple and effective method. Suppose he wants to go to Hawaii (travel within the United States), he merely checks with real estate associations until he finds one that's going to be in Hawaii. He registers for the convention (and pays the registration fee), goes to Hawaii, and never shows up for any of the business sessions.

This won't work on a foreign convention. In addition to the usual records for deductible expenses, the IRS requires a signed statement by the person who attended the foreign convention showing the number of days spent in attendance, the number of hours devoted to scheduled business activities, and a copy of the program. Then the IRS wants a signed statement from an officer of the sponsoring organization listing the business activities and attesting to the number of hours attended by the person seeking the deduction.

The government also tries to see to it that you don't live too well if you go to a foreign convention. For one thing, you can't fly first class and deduct the full cost unless there is no other way to fly: "The amount allowable as a deduction may not be more than the lowest coach or economy fare charged by any commercial airline for such transportation during the calendar month in which the convention begins. . . . If there is no coach or economy fare, then the lowest first class fare charged by any commercial airline is deductible."

That's not all, either. This deduction is allowed only if one-half or more of the days of the trip are devoted to business-related activities. If not, you can only deduct a portion based on the ratio of business days to total days in the trip. Travel time is not counted in the total.

Then there's a limit on the deduction of "subsistence expenses" such as food, lodging, tips, and local transportation. These are limited to the per diem amount established for United States government employees at the site of the convention. As you may recall from an earlier chapter, the government is not overly generous in establishing per diem rates.

In order to qualify for a full day's subsistence, there must be at least six hours of business scheduled by the convention, and you must attend at least two-thirds of the sessions. For a half-day's subsistence deduction, the convention must schedule at least three hours of business, and you must attend at least two-thirds of them.

Parties or dinners don't count as scheduled business-related activities, unless there's a speaker who talks on a business-related subject. Then you can count only the time "attributable" to the speech, which probably won't look too impressive on a time sheet, but based on my experience with after-dinner speakers, will seem interminable.

CHAPTER TEN

The Revenue Act of 1978

End of the Three-Martini Yacht

IN RESPONSE TO ALL THE NOISE about the three-martini lunch, Congress, in the final hectic hours of the 1978 session, passed a tax law which removed "entertainment facilities" from the tax deductible category. The law, however, left a lot of loose ends, some of which are expected to be tied together through a series of corrections of technical errors, and others which will probably have to be hacked out in the courts or in negotiations with the IRS.

This much is clear. A business that owns a yacht, hunting lodge, fishing camp, swimming pool, tennis court, or bowling alley will not be permitted to deduct depreciation charges or general operating costs such as rent, utility charges, repairs, insurance, and expenses for personnel servicing these facilities. The new law affects expenditures made after December 31, 1978, and presumably will apply to any money paid for the purchase of this type of facility in 1979 and thereafter.

It is also clear that interest, tax, and casualty losses on

entertainment facilities will still be deductible because these items are not subject to the entertainment facility rules.

Among the loose ends is the matter of dues for social, athletic, or sporting clubs. These are considered "entertainment facilities" for tax purposes, and while it appears to have been the intent of Congress to permit continued deductibility of these expenses, the law referred specifically to the "country club" as a "facility" that would remain deductible, and not to other clubs.

The legislative history went something like this: The Senate bill disallowed entertainment facility deductions, including club dues, while the House bill ignored the President's bid to crack down on business entertainment. In another section of the bill, the House proposed to tax unemployment insurance payments to upper income taxpayers (singles earning $20,000 a year or more and couples earning $25,000). This provision was not in the Senate version. There was a trade-off, with the Senate accepting the unemployment income tax and the House going along with the Senate's entertainment provision, except for club dues.

Congressional and Treasury aides, at a conference which lasted until 4:00 A.M. of adjournment day, said that they were convinced it was the intention of the conferees to preserve deductions for all business-related club dues. In the discussion, however, "country clubs" was used four out of five times and "club" only once. Thus, when the bill was drawn up to reflect the decision, the staff of the Joint Committee on Taxation used "country club."

The new Congress could correct the language, or the IRS might accept a broad interpretation of "country club." At the moment, however, Congressional amendment seems to have the best shot. There are thirty-two technical errors in the tax to be corrected, and the "club" oversight is among them.

House Democrat Dan Rostenkowski of Illinois, an old friend of golfing great Arnold Palmer, was credited with a key role in pushing the country club exemption. Congressman

Rostenkowski conceded that Palmer had called him several weeks before the House-Senate conference to urge that golf remain a deductible business expense. The Congressman added that he had been a long-time foe of the elimination of entertainment deductions because of the threat to the jobs of busboys, waiters, and kitchen help.

For its part, the IRS appears to be playing it straight. In the instructions for preparing 1978 returns, under entertainment facilities, the IRS inserted this very brief statement: "Beginning in 1979, you will no longer be able to deduct amounts paid or incurred for any entertainment facility, except for a country club."

The ban on deductibility of yachts and hunting lodges will not mean that business entertainment will be forever landlocked or that lovers of the hunt will have to give up pleasures of shooting deer (or each other) on an expense account. Joe D. Waggonner, Jr., a Louisiana Democrat who participated in the marathon conference, himself a hunting enthusiast, established during the discussion that the bill would not disturb the deductibility of hunting costs such as dogs, guides, licenses, and hunting rights.

The new law brought forth the usual spate of interpretations by accounting firms; and, generally, they concluded that out-of-pocket entertainment expenses incurred by taking a client on a hunting trip or on a boat trip would remain deductible, but the cost of renting the boat or the hunting lodge would not. For instance, Main Lafrentz and Company said, "If an executive takes a business associate hunting for a day, the expenses of the hunt, including meals, would be deductible provided that the current law substantiation requirements are met. However, if the hunters stayed overnight at a hunting lodge, the cost attributable to the lodging would be nondeductible."

Arthur Young and Company said, "As under prior law, out-of-pocket expenses incurred in connection with an entertainment activity involving the use of a facility are still deductible if they meet either the directly related or associated with tests. Thus, although the cost of renting a fishing boat to entertain a customer would not be deductible, the cost of food, beverages, and bait would be.''

Luncheon club costs remain deductible because they are not considered entertainment facilities. Business related expenses in professional associations and civic organizations were also undisturbed by the 1978 law.

The accounting firms' interpretations of what is and what is not deductible are based on two sections in the IRS instructions. One notes that out-of-pocket expenses for food, beverages, and other items furnished during business entertainment at a facility are not subject to facility rules, but rather must be judged by the rules for general entertainment. However, rent is included in the list of items subject to entertainment facility rules. While the ways of the tax man are mightily mysterious to us lay folk, it appears to me that if the entertainment is legitimately business oriented, there is no substantive reason why the cost of staying overnight at a hunting lodge or of renting a fishing boat should not be deductible.

The issue probably will not be decided before 1980, when the first returns based on the 1979 tax year will be filed. In the meantime, whichever way it goes, the expense account society will function under what amounts to a minor inconvenience.

CHAPTER ELEVEN

Executive Perks

Beating the Rising Cost of the Mercedes-Benz 280SE

THE IMPORTANCE OF PERKS and expense accounts cannot be overstated, especially during an inflationary period. The bleeding hearts have been giving us a lot of hogwash about how inflation hits hardest at the old and the poor. Actually, the real victims of inflation are corporate executives.

Consider the plight of the struggling executive who saw the price of a cashmere coat skyrocket from $200 to $350 in just three years. Or that of the CEO (Chief Executive Officer) living in Southern California or Fairfield County, Connecticut, where housing costs were rising at a rate of twenty-five percent a year.

Fortune magazine, which worries about the problems of the privileged, prepared an index of its own on the cost of living for the executive set and came up with numbers that would bring tears to the eyes of anyone but the most hardened Bolshevik. In an article called "Executives on the Inflation Treadmill" (Oct. 9, 1978), *Fortune* published a selected list of the expenditures appropriate to the lifestyle of upper-bracket executives, with estimates of price increases during the three year period ending June 1978.

The price of Chivas Regal scotch rose twenty-one percent; a bottle of Chateau Petrus '70 wine climbed twenty percent; a Mercedes-Benz 280SE soared fifty percent; and a Cadillac Sedan DeVille moved up twenty-two percent.

The cost of a nine-room suburban home shot up forty-seven percent; a thirty-three-foot Morgan sailboat was up thirty-six percent; a Piper Cherokee Warrior airplane rose twenty-four percent; tennis court rental, up eleven percent; dinner-theatre package, thirty-five percent; orchestra seats at the theatre, forty-six percent; annual country club dues, twenty-eight percent; trip to Europe, twenty-one percent—I could go on, but mercy restrains me.

However, all is not lost. Almost all of the above can be obtained as perks or on an expense account. The most common perk is the company automobile. Although prospectuses do not go out of their way to mention brand names, if you substitute Mercedes-Benz or Cadillac Sedan DeVille for "automobile," you'll come much closer to the full disclosure so dear to the Securities and Exchange Commission. As for housing, the company might supply a simple Park Avenue apartment or perhaps a couple of mansions.

Prior to 1978, executive perks were nobody's business but the executive's, his company's, and occasionally the IRS's. I say "occasionally" because as long as a perk is business related it is not taxable, and it's a fair assumption that executives are given perks so that they can function more effectively in going about their business. The IRS doesn't always buy this assumption. The IRS, however, is generally discreet in its dealings with taxpayers, and if there is a disagreement over whether a particular perk is taxable or not, the issue is worked out privately with the taxpayer.

The SEC, on the other hand, is a regulatory big-mouth, and one of its principal responsibilities is to see that corporations disclose to stockholders how corporate money is being spent.

After all, the stockholders are the owners of public corporations and are entitled to know what's happening to their money. So it was, that when a number of outrageous cases came to the attention of the SEC (the details of two particularly blatant ones will be reviewed in a subsequent chapter), the agency took action to bring the whole business of perks into the public domain.

In pressing for improved disclosure by business, for the benefit of investors or prospective investors, the SEC, on August 18, 1977, issued Interpretive Release No. 33-5856, in which, the commission said "personal benefits sometimes referred to as perquisites" must be included along with other remuneration to the highest paid officers and directors of public corporations.

The release threw the accounting world into a frenzy of activity as the major CPA firms rushed out bulletins to advise clients which perks needed to be disclosed and which could be omitted.

The SEC said that, in general, "incidental benefits which are ordinary or necessary to the conduct of company business, such as ordinary business lunches, and incidental payments made by the company for items which are directly related to the performance of management's functions at the company plant or offices, such as parking places, may not be reportable forms of remuneration. All payments made by the company for personal benefits received by management, which are not directly related to job performance, however, are forms of remuneration which should be included within the reported remuneration."

In other words, the SEC was saying that in proxy statements and other documents in which salaries and bonuses of top executives are reported, perks not directly tied to the performance of executives' jobs must also be included. The SEC wasn't passing judgment on the granting of various personal perks. It was merely requiring that stockholders be advised of these benefits.

Among the benefits which the commission classified as

remuneration that must be disclosed were the following: home repairs and improvements; housing and other living expenses, including domestic help provided at the executive's home or vacation residence; personal use of company automobiles, planes, yachts, apartments, hunting lodges, or company vacation houses; personal travel expenses; personal entertainment and related expenses; and legal, accounting, and other professional fees unrelated to business.

In addition, the SEC said that such items as low-cost bank loans, available to executives because the company may keep large balances at the bank; and special benefits from suppliers, stemming from corporate relationships, should also be included as remuneration.

On the question of expense accounts, the SEC said, "While itemized expense accounts may be considered job-related benefits whose value would be excluded from the aggregate remuneration reported, some may be forms of remuneration if they are excessive in amount or conferred too frequently." However, the SEC went on to say that the company would be in the best position to judge whether a form of compensation is remuneration, "based on the facts and circumstances involved in the situation." This leaves considerable room for individual interpretation.

The SEC also recognized that perks are often used to attract and hold the superior executives and noted that disclosure would not be required for "job-related benefits which are available to management employees generally, which do not relieve the individual of expenditures normally considered of a personal nature, and which are extended to management solely for the purposes of attracting and maintaining qualified personnel, facilitating their conduct of company business, or improving their efficiency in job performance."

In a later release (No. 33-5904, Feb. 6, 1978), the SEC answered specific questions on the more common perks. According to an analysis by Price Waterhouse and Company, here's the SEC position:

- Use of a company car or chauffeur-driven limousine for job-related transportation need not be disclosed, but personal use would constitute remuneration.
- Use of a company plane for commuting is part of an executive's compensation and "hitchhiking" on a company plane with empty seats would constitute payment even if there is no extra cost to the company. The cost of a commercial airline ticket for a similar flight might be used as a standard for determining the value to the executive.
- Use of company houses, apartments, yachts and the like for business purposes would not be considered remuneration. But if these facilities are used partially for business and the rest for personal use, there must be some form of allocation and personal benefits reported.
- Expenses of club memberships must also be allocated between business use and personal use, with the value of personal use reported.
- Physical examinations generally are not considered reportable income unless given at a resort, and tied in with a company-paid vacation, where the total cost is "disappropriate to the cost of a physical examination at a clinic or nonresort area."
- Broad-based life and health insurance plans provided by the company are not considered remuneration, but special insurance for executives, beyond that generally available, is.
- Professional services such as preparation of tax returns or wills also qualify as remuneration.

I think it's worth repeating that the SEC has no objection to perks as such but wants to make sure that nonbusiness-related perks, for executives whose remuneration must be disclosed, are included in the total.

In December 1978, the SEC issued new rulings that required public corporations to disclose salaries and other payments made to their five highest paid officers and directors who earned more than $50,000 a year. The old rules required only that the salaries of the three highest paid executives and directors making more than $40,000 be reported.

The new directive also provided for a tabular presentation of perks rather than the old footnote format, which stockholders and other normal beings tended to ignore. Footnotese is beyond the understanding of most English-speaking persons; so that type of presentation is more like a slow leak than full disclosure. This is not to say the footnote is being eliminated in dealing with perks. The tabular form will apply only if the perks do not exceed $25,000 or ten percent of total remuneration. Otherwise there must be detailed footnotes.

Under the December rules, some of the nit-picking is eliminated. The SEC now permits the exclusion from the reporting requirements of up to $10,000 in assorted perks that are difficult to track, such as the use of business cars.

The SEC wants perks disclosed, and the IRS wants them taxed; thus, with the help of its friends at the SEC, the IRS has a new source of information on executive perks.

The IRS has been taxing some perks for years, and the problem of distinguishing between business expenses and personal expenses has been a constant source of friction between taxpayers and the IRS. A further complication arises in trying to evaluate noncash, taxable benefits.

Many of the standards outlined by the SEC for determining reportable perks run parallel to IRS standards for taxable income, but there are some differences; Price Waterhouse has tabulated the respective positions of the two agencies on a number of the most commonly offered perks:

• On the use of company cars—with or without chauffeurs—first class travel on company business, company apartments, houses, country club memberships, professional organization fees, personal liability insurance premiums, and security devices in the home and/or bodyguards, the SEC position on remuneration and the IRS position on taxable income are essentially the same.

- The SEC considers "hitchhiking" on a company plane a form of remuneration, but a 1975 proposal by the IRS would not have taxed this perk, and, as of this writing, the IRS position is "uncertain."
- Company-paid life insurance is taxable except for the first $50,000 of group term insurance. The SEC is a little more liberal and exempts all company-paid life insurance available under a group plan to employees generally.
- Company-paid housing or other ordinary living expenses are considered remuneration by the SEC unless business related. The IRS says those perks are taxable unless the company's housing must be accepted as a condition of employment.
- As for low-interest or interest-free loans from the company or the company's bank, the SEC says they are reportable compensation if the terms are better than would be extended to a comparable borrower without the company connection. However, a tax court decision (35 TC 1083 [1961]) found an interest-free loan not taxable. The IRS disagrees with the tax court.
- Legal, financial and other personal, professional services are considered remuneration by the SEC, but such services, if related to tax liability or investment advice, are tax deductible.

If you're into studies, there was one undertaken by Martin E. Segal and Company, a New York-based consulting firm, on the most common perks. Using information covering reports on 1977 by 979 large corporations, the firm found that automobiles, club memberships, and company airplanes, in that order, head the list of perks. Some sixty-eight percent of the companies reporting on perks provide automobiles, forty-four percent provide club memberships, and sixteen percent, company planes.

Other perks, in descending order, are financial or tax counseling services; life insurance; low or no-cost loans; use of company products; medical expenses; provisions for the safety and security of executives and for their homes; and use of company-owned homes or apartments.

Statistically, the study found that, on the average, perks came to between 3 and 4 percent of the corporations' total compensation. The range was from a low of 0.6 percent to a high of 20.4 percent. Robert D. Paul, vice-president of the Segal firm, said that the figure on perks was "much less than we would have expected." He would not venture an opinion of what he would have expected.

Although the Segal study provided statistics on perks, the specifics are found in footnotes of proxy and registration statements made by corporations in their initial efforts to comply with the SEC's 1977 and 1978 disclosure requirements. Footnotes, formerly filled with technical trivia, came alive with tales of luxury living, corporate mansions, airplanes, resorts, and even a company-owned horse-breeding farm. There was also a rather feeble effort by some corporations to evaluate the slippery concept of nonbusiness-related perks. In the high-level corporate world there is no clear division between the person and the executive.

Generally, the perks were justified as "ordinary and incidental business expenses" paid for by corporations "in the interest of attracting and retaining qualified personnel, facilitating job performance, and minimizing the work-related expenses" of executives.

Skimming through excerpts from a fairly representative group of 1978 proxy statements, I found that most companies did not try to evaluate incidental personal benefits, and those that did came up with pretty small numbers. (Many of the specific examples were from data assembled by Deloitte Haskins and Sells, and Touche Ross and Company.) Most corporations reported that incidental personal benefits were "not practical to quantify," "not material," "extremely difficult to determine," "impossible to value," "not possible to estimate," etc.

General Telephone and Electronics, a communications giant

which reported sales in 1977 of $7,680,107,000, made a stab at evaluating personal benefits of perks and estimated that the nonbusiness-connected value of various perks "for all officers as a group in 1977 was less than $10,000."

CNA Financial, a major financial services corporation, was even stingier in providing personal benefits to its top officers or, at least, in its estimate of the value of the benefits. CNA said that its figures on remuneration included personal use or benefits of automobiles, club dues, and professional fees "which, in aggregate as to all officers and directors as a group, amounted to less than $2,300 in 1977."

Some companies used measures that appeared completely arbitrary. For instance, Oak Industries decided that twenty percent of the use of company cars, club memberships, and other perks resulted in personal benefits. It then estimated that the value of all those "indirect benefits does not exceed $13,000."

Union Bancorp, a large California-based, bank holding company, reported that it requires officers with company cars to reimburse the bank "a standard amount which the bank believes represents the average of personal usage." It does not disclose specifics of the "standard amount."

Another approach was taken by Ada Resources, a cattle, oil, and coal company headquartered in Houston, Texas. Ada, a relatively small company (fiscal 1978 sales, $102,340,000), reported that expenses for automobiles and for club memberships for all officers and directors came to $45,000 and added that the company did not require employees to keep records of personal use of the cars or club memberships.

As the rising cost of housing is a major area of executive concern, it is interesting to note how a number of executives apparently solved their housing problems. Hugh Hefner, the entrepreneur who parlayed the sexual revolution into a multimillion dollar empire, has his choice of two company-owned mansions—a fifty-four-room layout in Chicago with a twenty-room adjoining structure, and a twenty-nine room home in a Los Angeles suburb. According to Playboy's proxy material, the Chicago place is carried on the books at $2.9 million and the West Coast pad at $3.7 million. In fiscal 1977, it cost the company $700,000 to operate the Chicago residences and $1.9 million to run the one on the coast (including depreciation). For his part, Hefner pays the company $36,000 a year in rent for "the exclusive use of his personal quarters at the Los Angeles mansion and the non-exclusive use of other portions of the premises."

Playboy justifies company ownership and maintenance of this posh housing arrangement by pointing out that the mansions "are used in carrying on corporate activities, charitable functions, and a wide variety of promotional activities. The company believes that these operations are of substantial benefit to it and that they establish and increase public awareness and recognition of the company and its products and services. These operations are intended to, and in fact do, generate great publicity and recognition for the company, particularly with regard to maintaining and increasing circulation of the company's publications."

Playboy reports that the IRS is not in complete agreement with the company's interpretation and is, in fact, claiming that some of the expenditures, principally on the Los Angeles mansion, are not deductible. But Playboy is not knuckling under: "The company has vigorously challenged and protested the service's proposed assessment and believes that the expenditures are deductible. In years prior to fiscal 1970, the service allowed the deductibility of the expenditures for the Chicago mansion and the company maintains that the expenditures currently being challenged serve the same functions as the expenditures that have been allowed."

Columbia Pictures Industries reported that in fiscal 1977, it paid $66,600 to maintain a house in Beverly Hills for David Begelman, the controversial president of Columbia's motion picture operations (he lost his job in a check-forging scandal). Columbia said that at its request "the house has been used by

Mr. Begelman for a variety of business purposes including business entertainment and the screening of motion pictures. Inasmuch as the house has also been used by Mr. Begelman as a residence, Mr. Begelman pays a portion of the rent and other costs." Columbia did not say how much Begelman paid.

Atlantic Richfield, the big oil and mining company, gave its chairman an apartment in Los Angeles and provided him with a company plane for the commute between his New Mexico home and the company's offices. ARCO also maintained two houses in Las Cruces, Mexico.

If the automobile is the most common of executive perks, it is also the most difficult to quantify in terms of personal and business benefits. In a sample of various types of company disclosure reports, assembled by the accounting firm of Touche Ross and Company, about half of the twenty-six reports dealt with automobiles. Most of these said that the value of personal benefits of these automobiles was not included in calculating the total remuneration of officers and directors. Some gave reasons for failing to include these amounts; others merely made the statement and let it go at that.

However, Standard Prudential, a holding company in banking and commercial finance, reported that it furnished automobiles for five top officers and the net cost to the company of these automobiles ($13,161) for the year was included in the aggregate direct remuneration of the officers. There was no effort to separate business and personal use.

Glover, Incorporated, said the total salary it paid to key officers included "estimates of the value of the personal use of automobiles owned and maintained by the company." The amount of the estimates were not included.

Major League Bowling and Recreation, Incorporated, reported that the company provides cars for five officers, but there is no personal use of the cars.

More typical was The Seagram Company, which said that, "to assist their management functions," the company has furnished automobiles, drivers, and other transportation to three top officers. Remuneration reported for these officers "does not include the economic benefit of any use of such transportation which may be deemed to be non-business connected."

Shaw Industries said it did not include the value of the use of company automobiles because management could not determine the value. Tyco Laboratories and Marathon Manufacturing also noted that they couldn't calculate the value of personal use.

Among the more elaborate disclosures was one by Harrah's, the splashy Nevada gaming operation. It reported that in 1977 officers and directors received an assortment of benefits, such as the personal use of corporate entertainment facilities and vehicles, and payment for personal travel, entertainment, and professional services. The company pointed out that it was difficult to identify and evaluate these personal services, but estimated that the whole deal came to about $23,000 for the year ending June 30. 1977.

Harrah's also disclosed that it was having some differences of opinion with the tax people. The IRS had disallowed deductions of $88,765, taken by the company on its 1974 federal tax return, for corporate aircraft use and other travel expenses of William F. Harrah, founder, chief executive officer, and owner of eighty percent of the company's stock (Mr. Harrah died in June of 1978). The company went along with $51,121 of the IRS claim but disputed the rest.

For fiscal 1977, Mr. Harrah paid the company $22,467 for what he and the company agreed was his personal portion of corporate aircraft expenses. However, Harrah's said there was no way of knowing whether the IRS would go along with this evaluation.

Although it's down toward the bottom of the list of perks, low-cost or no-cost loans can help pave the way for an executive to pick up an ownership interest in his company or perhaps buy a house suitable to his station in life. At Heublein, the company provided guarantees on loans for key executives totaling $3 million so they could purchase Heublein stock. In addition to the guarantee, the company agreed to pay any interest costs above six percent (the loans were at seven percent as of August 31, 1977). Heublein reported that it normally keeps large balances at the bank involved, and at the time of the disclosure had about $1.2 million in deposits at that bank.

International Harvester lent its president $1.8 million at six percent so he could buy 60,000 shares of International Harvester stock. MCA, the movie and television production company, lent its president $700,000 at four percent for a "personal residence."

While horse racing and horse boarding privileges will not be found among the top ten on the perk-popularity charts, Frisch's Restaurants disclosed that its president, Jack C. Maier, ran a horse-breeding and boarding operation at a company-owned farm near Cincinnati. The company explained that it used the farm for "public relations purposes" and the horses there were "a featured attraction for visitors."

Apparently, the IRS wasn't too crazy about this arrangement, and in auditing the company's returns for 1973 through 1975 indicated that it thought that $462,800 deducted by the company should be allocated to Mr. Maier's horse operations and that the IRS planned to assess the company $222,000 in taxes and $270,000 in penalties.

The company said that, as a result of the IRS audit, it had determined that Mr. Maier was not charged $158,929 for expenses in racing his horses. It was also determined that the company failed to charge him $29,625 for boarding horses. "These undercharges were without the knowledge of Mr. Maier and other members of the board of directors and resulted from errors by company bookkeeping and farm personnel in allocating expenses and reporting the number of horses on the farm."

Mr. Maier has repaid the company $188,554 plus eight

percent interest, or $17,883. Since May 30, 1976, he has been paying the company for expenses related to his horses and horses boarded for other owners.

The treatment of rides on company aircraft remains a matter of confusion. The SEC says that even if there is no extra cost to the company in permitting employees and their families to hitch a ride on a company plane, the cost of comparable commercial air transportation should be considered remuneration. The IRS position is ambiguous. In 1975, the IRS proposed that "hitchhiking" on a company plane should not be considered taxable income.

Corporate management is clearly opposed to charging an executive for a flight if there is no cost to the company. Atlantic Richfield took this position, stating, "The company permits officers, directors, and other employees and their guests to occupy seats on company aircraft that would otherwise remain empty when such aircraft are on business trips. The company believes that the incremental cost to it of providing such transportation is insignificant and that such use of company aircraft by officers, directors, and other employees should not be considered to constitute remuneration to them; although it is aware that the staff of the Securities and Exchange Commission has stated a contrary view. The company has not maintained detailed records of such travel; however, it estimates that the total value of all such usage (measured by commercial air fare schedules) for all officers and directors as a group would range from $85,000 to $100,000 for 1977."

On the same subject, General Tire and Rubber says that it is company policy to permit employees using company planes on business trips to take along immediate families or guests with no charge, "provided that they occupy seats that otherwise would go unused."

International Paper reported that company planes are used for business and that "any personal use is rare and requires both senior executive approval and reimbursement of the company's costs."

Vulcan, Incorporated, said that its company airplane is occasionally used for personal purposes when this "will not interfere with the company's business," and only with the approval of the chief executive officer. Vulcan's policy is to require reimbursement for any extra cost to it.

In its report on payments to top executives, Ford Motor Company said that its totals did not include "various items which may have been of some personal benefit" but which the company considered essentially business related and which "involve little or no additional company cost. These, according to Ford, included cars, drivers, spaces on company planes on business trips, hotel accommodations on a space-available basis at facilities maintained for business purposes, and incidental personal use of company telephones.

Said Ford, "The company does not have a reasonable basis for determining the cost or value of any personal benefit that may be involved, but believes they are neither excessive nor unusual."

That's what Ford said, but that's not what a couple of stockholders' suits filed in 1978 said. These suits charged Henry Ford II, chairman, and his "rubber stamp" board of directors with massive waste of corporate assets. The suits focused principally on Mr. Ford and accused him of all manner of personal extravagances at company expense: use of the corporate aircraft to vacation with a "close intimate friend" (female), heavy corporate expenditures for his personal living quarters, and personal use of a fleet of corporate limousines. The actions even accused the multimillionaire executive of accepting bribes and kickbacks for corporate favors, and accused the company of making illegal payments to obtain a foreign contract.

Mr. Ford and the Ford Company have denied the charges, and at this writing the case remains unresolved. More specifically, the following was charged:

• Mr. Ford received a $750,000 kickback in exchange for a contract granting exclusive rights for vending machine installations at Ford company facilities. Mr. Ford allegedly diverted the money into a Swiss bank account.

- The Ford Company made $1,889,000 in illegal payments in connection with a contract for a communications system in Indonesia.
- Mr. Ford was paid $2 million in cash by the wife of the president of the Phillippines in exchange for locating a Ford stamping plant there. The plant cost the company $50 million and lost money at an annual rate of $17 million.
- Mr. Ford enjoyed a string of perks ranging from the aircraft, apartments, and limousines to an annual bird hunting trip to Scotland.

The lawyers in the case were of the high-powered variety. Representing the plaintiffs was Saxe, Bacon and Bolan, in which the former whiz-kid, Roy M. Cohn, is a partner. Representing the Ford interests were Paul, Weiss, Rifkind and Garrison; Huges, Hubbard and Reed; Shea, Gould, Climenko and Casey; and Wachtell, Lipton, Rosen and Katz, all among New York's most prestigious firms.

Details of the charges against Mr. Ford were laid out in a 104-page document, *Answers to Interrogatories,* as part of the pre-trial maneuvering in which lawyers for opposing sides try to get details in order to prepare for trial. The questions were posed by the Ford attorneys, and the answers were attested to by I. Walton Bader, a New York attorney whose law firm was one of the suing stockholders. The point of the questions was to obtain specifics on the general allegations made in the New York State Supreme Court action, and some of the answers were pretty specific.

The plaintiffs said that Mr. Ford used a corporate plane to transport personal furniture to his overseas homes and the home of

his close personal friend Kathy DuRoss. Specifically, the company's corporate aircraft was deployed and used solely to transport an ornate fireplace that Mr. Ford had purchased for Miss DuRoss. The company's corporate aircraft have also been used at the direction of Henry Ford II to transport Josephine Ford's pet dogs and cats from location to location whenever she felt her pets were in need of a change of climate. At the direction of Mr. Ford, corporate aircraft were used to transport caviar, Dom Perignon champagne, Chateau Lafite wine, and a special lean bacon for his personal use from location to location. In fact, Mr. Ford deploys corporate aircraft to maintain his supply of caviar at his office and residences as if the company ran a New York to Detroit air shuttle.

. . . On one recent return flight from Europe, Mr. Ford, at the behest of his guest, made an unscheduled stop to purchase a single pack of cigarettes, which stop Henry Ford II was quoted as saying cost $6,000.

More recently, the court papers note, Ford used company aircraft to fly himself and his "close intimate friend, Kathy DuRoss," on a vacation from London to Palma, Mallorca.

Mr. Ford, according to the stockholders' account, had six to nine corporate limousines and drivers at his disposal in New York for his personal use and for the use of his family and friends. The number of limos was said to have been reduced to three after the suit was filed.

Corporate limousines driven by corporate employees are made available to Miss DuRoss as a regular proposition including, but not limited to, family events of the DuRoss family in which limousines owned by Ford Motor Company and driven by Ford Motor Company employees are placed at the disposal of Miss DuRoss and members of her family.

[When Miss DuRoss's father died] the company limousines and personnel lined the street in front of 856 Hampton Road, Grosse Pointe Woods, Michigan, which house was purchased for the DuRoss family by Henry Ford II. Additionally, company limousines and personnel were used for the wedding of Kathy DuRoss's daughter . . .

The stockholders' statement accused Mr. Ford of having an

"insatiable desire for personal extravagance and convenience" and cited the following as examples:

- An apartment at the Carlyle Hotel in New York which was off limits to other corporate executives even though the company paid the $80,340 a year in maintenance charges on it. In all, over $1 million was spent by the company in connection with the apartment. The Ford Company also maintained apartments at the Waldorf and Ritz Hotels for corporate business. (Mr. Ford purchased the six-room duplex at the Carlyle in 1970 for $352,000 and sold it in 1977, according to the *Wall Street Journal*.)
- Sauna baths that cost $250,000.
- A private gymnasium and full-time masseur.
- A private dining room, staffed by six full-time employees, including a Swiss chef. Each meal served was estimated to cost the company $200.
- Spiral staircases to connect his tower facilities at Detroit's Renaissance Plaza with a suite for Mr. Ford's afternoon rest. The staircases and related decoration were estimated to cost $2,700,000.
- The Presidential Suite at the Hyatt Regency Hotel maintained on a preemptive basis for Mr. Ford's exclusive use. The Hyatt Regency facility is so close to the Renaissance Plaza "that Mr. Ford could probably reach the Presidential Suite by sliding down the $2,700,000 staircase."

The stockholders further contended that the company maintained "elaborate" living quarters for executives at the Grosvenor House in London; yet Mr. Ford stayed at his own mansion in London and billed the company $300 for every night he slept at his own house. Also, Mr. Ford "caused the company to purchase," for $10 million, a house on Grafton Street in London which "serves no corporate purpose."

Additional misuse of assets, the plaintiffs said,

occurs on an annual basis when Henry Ford II has the company pick up the tab for bird hunting in Scotland for Mr. Ford and his friends. No less than ten company cars and drivers are required on such outings to accommodate the whim of Mr. Ford and his guests. Needless to say, these guests further receive free room and meals during their stay, compliments of the company's stockholders, even though the stockholders are uninformed about this.

During the fall of 1977, Henry Ford II directed the expenditure of $300,000 in corporate funds in order to cover the cost of a party for the governors of the fifty states. Invitations from the Ford family, specifically Henry Ford II, William Ford, Benson Ford, and Josephine Ford, cordially invited the governor of each and every state to attend a personal party at Henry Ford II's mother's house. Thirty-two governors accepted with a cost factor to the company's shareholders of approximately $9,400 per governor. This expenditure was concealed as "renovations."

The suing stockholders also contend that credit card use for personal calls by Mr. Ford and his family costs the company between $50,000 and $100,000 a year. Then the complainants come in with the ultimate insult:

> Upon information and belief, the defendant Henry Ford II performs little, if any, services of value to the company. Indeed, he was just named by a leading business publication as one of the ten worst executives in the country.

Attacking the board of directors, the court papers noted:

> Henry Ford II was and still is the principal beneficiary of said conspiracy; however, each and every defendant who is a director of the company as set forth in Exhibit A to the complaint benefited from said conspiracy in that upon agreeing to serve on the company's rubber stamp board of directors, each director receives anywhere from $30,000 to $50,000 per year (depending upon committee fees), Dom Perignon champagne, two automo-

biles, and through the courtesy of the non-consenting stock-holders, a life insurance policy with a face value of $250,000.

Whatever Mr. Ford's qualifications are as a chief executive officer, he's in little danger of losing his job unless the Ford family wants him out. (He has resigned as chief executive officer of the company.) The family owns virtually all 14,634,759 shares of class B stock which represent forty percent of the voting stock of the company. Although there are 104 million shares of class A stock, class A shares have one vote apiece while class B shares have 4.732 votes. Thus, the descendants of founder Henry Ford are able to control forty percent of the vote with about thirteen percent of the stock.

CHAPTER TWELVE

Jerome Castle

Carrying a Good Thing Too Far

WITH SO MUCH CASH generated by large corporations, and with a tendency by officers and directors to confuse management with ownership, it's not surprising that some top executives get carried away and go well beyond the pleasures of perks that are legitimately available.

At least two blatant cases of perk abuse came to the attention of the SEC, and as a result of proceedings before that agency, many of the details have become part of the public record. One, which spawned a criminal action, had, as its central personality, Jerome Castle, who after a proxy fight in 1967 captured control of Penn-Dixie Industries, a $280 million-a-year cement, steel, and construction company. As of the end of 1977, Castle personally held 5.4 percent of Penn-Dixie's common stock. In addition to claims that he wasted $1.7 million of the company's money on high living, Castle was accused of participating in or condoning various frauds that further bilked the company.

The central figure in the other case was Victor Posner, an entrepreneur of unquestioned ability, who controls an industrial empire with a combined volume of about $1 billion a year. Mr. Posner and his family were cited by the SEC for personal use of corporate assets, and the whole affair was settled by the payment of about $1.7 million back to the corporations. We will go into the Posner case in the next chapter, but first, Mr. Castle.

Jerome Castle, a handsome man with thick black hair and intense eyes, turned up in the securities business in 1967 when Wall Street was obsessed with corporate takeovers. He was thirty-two years old and worked as an arbitrageur, looking for opportunities to make money out of the spread between prices of securities to be exchanged in pending merger negotiations. Swept up in the tide of the times, he joined a group formed to launch a proxy fight to take control of Penn-Dixie. The group was successful, collecting 1.3 million shares for their slate of directors against 1.1 million for the incumbents, and in August of 1967, Castle emerged as chief executive officer.

Operations at Penn-Dixie moved along fairly well in the early years of Castle's regime, but in 1975 the company began losing money heavily. By 1977, the losses had reached $15 million; trading in Penn-Dixie stock was suspended by the New York Stock Exchange in April 1977 and didn't resume until December 1978. The company appeared to be headed for the financial rocks. Castle was fired in mid-1977 as a corporate scandal blossomed.

The SEC brought its regulatory force into the Penn-Dixie case with the filing of a complaint on November 16, 1976, which included charges of a $6 million Florida land deal fraud. The Florida deal became the subject of criminal charges brought against Castle and others by a federal grand jury in New York on October 10, 1978.

It was charged, that with Castle's connivance, Penn-Dixie paid $6 million to one of his business buddies for the swampy portion of a 12,500 acre tract in Florida. The seller bought the entire parcel for $5.7 million just one day before the sale to

Penn-Dixie of forty-four percent of it, and concealed his identity through use of a Cayman Island trust. In addition to being under water, the land was said to be next to a navy bombing range and had a geological fault running through its middle.

The SEC proceeding was worked out by a consent decree entered in July of 1977, which provided that special counsel, hired in April of that year by Penn-Dixie to investigate indications of hanky-panky, should push his probe and submit a report for review by an audit committee. The report, by New York attorney Gary P. Naftalis, provided a blow-by-blow description of personal indulgence and corporate rape. It also made a series of recommendations for tightening up the operation.

In general, the special counsel found "a pervasive pattern of wrongful conduct which harmed Penn-Dixie." The prime beneficiaries were Castle and Arnold Y. Aronoff, a co-defendant in the criminal case as a principal in the land swindle. Aronoff pleaded guilty in May of 1979.

Aronoff was an officer of one of Penn-Dixie's large cement customers and allegedly participated in some of the other questionable transactions unearthed by the special counsel. The report concluded the following about Castle:

- He was either a participant in or "reckless facilitator" of the Florida land scheme.
- He secretly caused Penn-Dixie to enter into a long-term contract to supply cement at low prices to Edward C. Levy Company, where Aronoff, son-in-law of Edward C. Levy, Sr., was a vice-president. (Penn-Dixie lost an estimated $2,795,000 on the deal.)
- He was largely responsible for $320,000 in improper secret payments and finder's fees to Aronoff, and "commissions" to Aronoff's father.
- He misappropriated more than $1.7 million in corporate assets for his own use between 1971 and 1977.
- He caused Penn-Dixie to contribute $544,750 to a founda-

tion which he used primarily as a vehicle to purchase Penn-Dixie stock and assure his continued control of the company.

- He caused Penn-Dixie and Castle Capital (a leasing subsidiary) to buy worthless securities from him and his associates.
- He dissipated assets by causing Castle Capital to make wasteful investments in race horses and loans to associates. (Castle Capital also invested $2 million in a posh jet set restaurant on Madison Avenue in New York called La Folie, which has been a consistent money-loser.)
- He misled the SEC, Penn-Dixie's auditors, and the special counsel.

Special counsel Naftalis said he found no direct evidence that Castle benefited from the Florida swamp transaction, but noted that after preliminary interviews, Castle refused to cooperate further.

Aronoff was able to pull off the land caper, according to the special counsel's report, by supplying false appraisals, feasibility studies, and letters designed to create the impression that Penn-Dixie could quickly resell the land at a profit. He concealed his interest and the fact that he had acquired the entire parcel for a lower price a day before the Penn-Dixie sale.

According to the special counsel, Aronoff controlled the sources of information about the land. He recommended the appraiser and the consulting firm that did the development study and had a hand in selecting the Florida attorney who represented Penn-Dixie:

> Mr. Aronoff provided the developer, Edward J. Robinson [also indicted], who contacted Penn-Dixie on behalf of a non-existent group that proposed buying the land from Penn-Dixie. Mr. Aronoff also told Mr. Robinson the price he should offer Penn-Dixie and then allowed Mr. Aronoff's name to be included in

the developer's fictitious purchasing group. Moreover, Mr. Aronoff arranged bank financing for Penn-Dixie, and his agents and lawyer formed a company to manage and maintain Penn-Dixie's property.

The report goes on to conclude that the fraud could not have gone through without Mr. Castle's participation or his acting in a "faithless and reckless" manner:

> Special counsel found substantial evidence that Mr. Castle was aware that Mr. Aronoff was the seller of the land; he was aware that the land to be acquired by Penn-Dixie was primarily swamp land; he misled Penn-Dixie's directors, bankers, and independent accountants as to a number of matters relating to Penn-Dixie's acquisition of the land; and his account of the transaction to special counsel was not truthful. Special counsel also found that Mr. Castle made no effort to verify any of the information provided to Penn-Dixie through the efforts of Mr. Aronoff, and he disregarded the negative judgments of the two Penn-Dixie employees who had actually seen the land or reviewed available information about it.

The biggest part of the $1.7 million which Castle appropriated for himself was spent on cushy living quarters. The company paid $1,261,528 on the Hampshire House suite on Central Park South in New York City; $41,505 for temporary quarters at the Waldorf during the renovation of the Hampshire House; and $36,314 for an apartment and suites at various clubs in Bal Harbour, Florida.

The Hampshire House apartment was put together by combining three apartments. The suite was then "lavishly furnished and decorated." The company paid $187,000 to buy the three apartments; another $124,393 for antiques and art work; $172,880 for furniture, carpets, and wall coverings; and $383,349 for renovation. Castle made all the decisions on the decor. In connection with the antiques, the probe came up with an interesting sidelight; they were copies. In a footnote, the report said the following:

> Frederick P. Victoria, the decorator who selected and purchased most of the antiques at the Hampshire House on Penn-Dixie's behalf, refused to allow us to interview him. Victoria received a total of $795,709.50 from Penn-Dixie between 1970 and 1977, approximately $500,000 for work on the corporate apartment, and approximately $300,000 for work on the corporate office. Mr. Victoria's refusal to be interviewed is particularly disturbing in light of the recent disclosure that the antiques which he purchased for Penn-Dixie are, in reality, only copies.

On top of the original investment in the suite, maintenance charges totaled $296,624 from June 1971 through June 1977. Another $28,293 went for maids, housekeepers, butlers, and cooks who essentially served Castle personally; $43,708 for food, liquor, and dry cleaning; and $12,260 for cable television and repairs to Castle's stereo system.

The special counsel's report quoted Castle as stating that the Hampshire House apartments were necessary as offices, that he seldom spent his evenings there, and that many others with valid business reasons stayed at the suite.

The report "did not uncover any credible corroboration of Castle's statements." The evidence pointed to his use of the suite as a personal residence. Various Hampshire House employees said that Castle, his wife, and his personal staff were the only ones who slept there; his laundry and mail were regularly delivered there; his announcement of his third wedding gave the apartment as his address; and the wedding ceremony was held there.

The special counsel gave no weight to logs that were supposed to show who used the apartment "because they show no use at all by Castle during evenings, when even Castle admitted to us that he used the apartment, albeit he claimed he did so infrequently."

Further puncturing Castle's argument that the suite served

as a corporate office, the report quoted a corporate officer who said he wouldn't schedule meetings at the apartment because he feared "interrupting some personal activity of Castle's."

Even if it were an office, the report contended, there was no need for it. Between 1969 and 1971, Penn-Dixie spent over $1.5 million to decorate offices at 1345 Avenue of the Americas, only seven blocks from the Hampshire House. "These offices were as luxurious and large as any business of Penn-Dixie's size could have needed. Castle's own office there was over 1,200 square feet. Company officials other than Castle were content to use their regular offices and the readily available conference rooms. Indeed, since Castle resigned as president of Penn-Dixie in May 1977, no one has used the Hampshire House apartment."

The Waldorf-Astoria apartment was rented for about six months in 1971 while the Hampshire House suite was being decorated. While Castle would not talk about the reason for the Waldorf suite, other officers told the investigators that the only reason for renting it was to provide Castle a place to live. "The personal use was so blatant that a log was not even kept."

Castle's Bal Harbour, Florida, apartment cost the company $30,700 between 1973 and October 1977. During the same period the company spent an additional $6,014 for suites at various clubs in the Miami area—Jockey Club, Palm Bay Club, and Playboy Plaza. The special counsel concluded,

> There was no legitimate business purpose for Penn-Dixie to have a Florida apartment or suite. Its divisions did little or no business in Florida. The apartments were not used enough for business purposes, and they did not qualify for the deduction as an entertainment facility under IRS guidelines.
>
> At least by 1976, Castle seems to have recognized that Penn-Dixie's paying for the apartment might not be proper. To cover it up, in October of that year, he ordered the steel division, which was headquartered in Kokomo, Indiana, and had no use for the apartment, to pay for it. The apartment had been

previously paid for by the New York office. This change concealed the payment for some time from Penn-Dixie's auditors.

It is clear, the special counsel asserted, that the Bal Harbour
apartment served as Castle's winter home.

Then there were the obligatory corporate aircraft. Penn-
Dixie leased a jet and a helicopter from Castle Capital and
logs were kept of the use of the planes. The logs showed three
flights to a Long Island beach resort by Castle and friends and
over 200 flights to and from south Florida with few mentions
of Castle as a passenger. However, those who were listed told
investigators that Castle was on the Florida flights "very
often."

The special counsel decided that there was no business
justification for most of the Florida flights, and that they
served merely to shuttle Castle between company locations and
his winter home. Other flights which appeared to lack business purposes were five trips to Las Vegas and to the Bahamas.
Passengers on the flights confirmed that there was no business
reason for them.

The plane was also used to transport politicians and
celebrities. One was a presidential candidate flown several
times between New Hampshire and Florida in 1972, just
before the presidential primaries in those states. (The special
counsel declined to disclose the name of the candidate, but
you can bet he was a Democrat. One of the minor personal
expenses paid by Penn-Dixie for Castle was $918 in dues to
the National Democratic Club over the years 1971-77.)

A Penn-Dixie lawyer was shocked at the blatant non-
business use of the airplane and suggested that the company
stop listing the names of celebrities on the logs. Instead, it was
suggested that when Castle wanted to transport these types, he
should arrange for a Penn-Dixie customer to requisition the
plane. Then Castle could take anyone he wanted, not list their
names, and simply label the trip "customer entertainment."
While no one would admit that this advice was followed,

these names stopped appearing on the logs the year this lawyer joined the company. In all, the special counsel estimated Castle owed the company $156,276 for misuse of corporate aircraft.

Turning its attention to improvements at Castle's Glen Cover, Long Island, home, the special counsel's report focused on $24,579 spent for a fence and security system; $12,300 to build a tennis court; and $11,776 for a forty-foot stainless steel flagpole.

The fence and security system were the "most expensive of their kind" and a Penn-Dixie officer sought to justify the expenditure as a plan by Penn-Dixie to develop and market security related items. Although there was some evidence that Penn-Dixie was trying to get into the security business, Castle's property was never used for demonstration or marketing purposes. James Morrill, head of the steel division, who originally had said the fence was part of a marketing plan, later admitted that Castle's place was too far removed from any possible business source to be used effectively in marketing. The report added the following:

> Morrill's purported justification must also be viewed in the light of the fact that he too had the steel division erect a chain link fence around his own farm, located in an area of upstate New York, even more remote in terms of possible promotional use than was Castle's Glen Cove property.

There was also an effort to justify the tennis court as business related. Two cement division officials said that they were experimenting with the properties of a cement designed to resist cracking in cold climates. They could not explain why the testing should be done in Glen Cove, Long Island, so far removed from Penn-Dixie's cement or laboratory facilities. Instructions to build the tennis court came from the "Executive Committee of the Cement Division," an entity which appeared to be nonexistent.

The $11,776 flagpole, which the special counsel said served no business purpose and "merely assisted Castle in celebrating the nation's bicentennial," became something of a problem. After the company's outside auditors discovered the payment and Castle realized he could never justify it from a business point of view, he tried to unload it. He wrote a memo to Penn-Dixie's construction division in Albany, New York, offering to give them the pole.

Special counsel noted, "The construction division had never shown any prior interest in obtaining such a flagpole. Moreover Castle never subsequently communicated with the division about the matter, and to the best of our knowledge, the flagpole remains at Glen Cove." Anyone looking for a forty-foot, stainless steel flagpole used only once every two-hundred years, please contact the above.

Another personal service which the special counsel charged was provided for Castle at company expense was an "all around man" and a maid who worked at Castle's Glen Cove home.

In the area of T&E, Castle ran up bills totaling $109,496 from 1971 through 1977, which the special counsel called "unsubstantiated." Penn-Dixie had house accounts at several expensive restaurants where Castle frequently dined, and in one year, 1973, these bills came to $51,976. There were instances in which Castle told other employees to cover his restaurant expenses by submitting expense sheets, with their names, for meals he had eaten.

Besides using house accounts, Castle took advances for expenses and didn't worry too much about accounting for the money. "Years later he would submit several years worth of expense account forms, with virtually no receipts or other underlying documents to substantiate the expenses. For example, in 1971, he submitted reports for the years 1968 through 1971. Between 1968 and 1977, Castle received over $109,000 as reimbursement or advances, an average of almost $11,000 per year."

In addition to supporting Castle in style, Penn-Dixie also

provided payments of about $40,000 for two of Castle's former wives. A payment of $22,500 was made in 1970 to Carole Belcher Interiors for decorating services at Penn-Dixie's Chicago office. Carole Belcher was Castle's second wife. The special counsel said, "The available evidence shows that the payment should not have been made. The Chicago office was decorated only sparsely, therefore making it very doubtful that any substantial services were actually performed. Moreover, on the day before the payment was made, Castle wrote a memorandum which noted the possible need for disclosure of the payment in Penn-Dixie's proxy statement because of Carole's relationship to Castle. No such disclosure was ever made."

The other payments, $15,000 and $4,234, made in 1973 and 1974 to Castle's third wife, were for services she apparently rendered—designing a corporate logo and doing public relations work. However, the special counsel said the payments to the third Mrs. Castle created "the appearance of impropriety."

In one section of the special counsel's report, Castle is accused of outright theft in connection with the reimbursement of proxy-fight expenses leading to control of Penn-Dixie. One of Castle's chief allies during the contest was repaid $93,111 by Penn-Dixie for expenses (in proxy fights the winner's expenses are repaid by the company). In 1976, Castle's colleague filed a sworn statement with the IRS that the expenses totaled that amount, but substantiating records for part of the outlays had been accidently destroyed.

In an interview with the special counsel, the Castle ally "admitted he and Castle had inflated the amount . . . and divided the excess, and also admitted that no substantiating records had been destroyed because they never existed." The counsel's report called the scheme "nothing less than theft" and recommended that Penn-Dixie try to get back from Castle $16,000 in unsubstantiated proxy expenses.

Additional allegations of questionable corporate expenditures involved $261,992 paid for bodyguard service. Castle, the report said, had a "deeply ingrained fear of bodily injury" as a result of a beating he was given during a labor dispute in 1969, and he employed bodyguard service twenty-four hours a day, seven days a week. The representative of the security service also served as Castle's gofer. The special counsel observed: "Whether or not Castle was justified in having Penn-Dixie pay for a personal bodyguard in 1969 (the year he was beaten), our investigation did not discover evidence to support that expenditure over the entire eight years that followed." Neither was there any justification for using the bodyguard as a "personal servant," the special counsel added.

Another matter which came to the attention of the investigators was the expenditure of $7,209 of Penn-Dixie's money on three trips Castle made to Europe (one of which included the rental of a yacht for $5,525). An effort was made to justify the yachting trip as a possible aid to Castle's health, which in turn might have helped Penn-Dixie's financial health. "We do not doubt that Castle felt healthier as a result of the trip, but we cannot conclude that that fact justifies the payments. The company's financial health seems not to have been helped thereby," said the special counsel in a rare burst of drollery.

There were, of course, charges of personal use of corporate limousine service, and while the records appeared to be inaccurate and witnesses told of "extensive personal use" of limousines by Castle, the special counsel was unable to nail down a figure covering Castle's personal obligation on that score.

Finally, there was a question of $6,500 given to Castle by the company to reimburse him for an advance he was supposed to have made to a customer while both were in Las Vegas. The company controller of that period said he understood that Castle had actually used the money to gamble. However, no other evidence was uncovered relating to the gambling theory.

Although the report said that Castle bore most of the responsibility for the misuse of the $1.7 million in Penn-Dixie money, the special counsel took a strong swipe at two other officers: "Almost all of the instances of misconduct, however, required the active collusion of either Harvey Kushner, executive vice-president, or James Jacobsen, chief financial officer. Both men were also directors of Penn-Dixie." (Neither is with the company any longer, although Kushner served briefly as acting chief executive officer after the ouster of Castle.)

Written approval of two executives was required before a check could be issued, the report said:

> Castle, thus, could not make payments for his personal benefit without help, and indeed, Castle seldom approved payments to anyone. Kushner and/or Jacobsen approved most of the payments for Castle's personal benefit, including almost all of the extravagant decorating, incidental food, and other bills associated with the Hampshire House apartments. It is significant that they approved the Hampshire House expenditures with knowledge that Castle used the apartments as his personal residences. The same was true of the various Florida apartments. They knew Castle used the apartments as his winter residences; yet they authorized the payments anyway. They both authorized the enormous payments for the bodyguards even though, as Kushner admitted, he knew Castle used the bodyguards as gofers. Jacobsen was at the board meeting of Penn-Dixie at which installation of the perimeter fence and security system around Castle's Glen Cove property was approved. Both Kushner and Jacobsen admitted knowing that Castle had submitted three years of alleged expenses, without adequate substantiation, some three years after Castle had incurred the last expense; yet they permitted Penn-Dixie to reimburse Castle and to grant him advances.

Other lower level employees knew of Castle's misuse of funds but had little power to stop the practice. "However, there is, in our opinion, no such excuse for high level executives like Kushner and, to a lesser extent, Jacobsen, who not only had detailed knowledge of Castle's practices but actively aided Castle in misappropriating the company's funds."

The report concluded that Kushner, who was paid $351,250 in 1975 including bonuses and stock (Castle received $725,000 in salary and bonuses that year), "did not want to lose his own very good job." As to Jacobsen, the report said, his motives were more difficult to determine. Perhaps, "Jacobsen, like Castle, was unable to distinguish between personal and company affairs."

Aside from the $1.7 million in allegedly misused assets, the special counsel found a number of other Castle capers of more than passing interest. For example, about a year after gaining control of the company, Castle (technically Penn-Dixie) organized the Penn-Dixie Foundation as a charitable organization. In 1969 he changed the name to the Jerome Castle Foundation and has maintained control with himself, his former wife, and his aunt as trustees.

The company poured $544,750 into the foundation, but just a small portion of the money was used for contributions. One contribution was $16,000 to the school where Mr. Castle's children were enrolled. The bulk of the money, or about $438,000, was used to buy 74,000 shares of Penn-Dixie stock and thus helping Castle maintain control of the company. The foundation also purchased a painting for $21,000 which found its way into Castle's New York apartment and later into La Folie, the deluxe, Madison Avenue restaurant owned by Castle Capital.

The decor at La Folie features thirteen malachite pilasters, nine feet high by fourteen inches wide, created by a Long Island artist, Stephen Lipkins, for $4,500 each. Mr. Lipkins, one of a handful of Americans fabricating mosaic designs out of the green, gemlike mineral, said the LaFolie assignment was the biggest job he had ever done, and represented the only work of its kind "this side of the Hermitage Museum in Leningrad."

Although Castle Capital was 79.8 percent owned by Penn-

Dixie, the special counsel listed a series of transactions in which Castle Capital appeared to be ripping off its parent. (Castle Capital's only new leases since 1973 were with Penn-Dixie.) For one, Penn-Dixie Steel was about to purchase a building for expanded office space when Castle Capital bought it instead and leased it to Penn-Dixie for about $1.4 million more than it would have cost Penn-Dixie to buy the building. In addition, Penn-Dixie paid all the acquisition expenses and more than $100,000 to renovate the building. For another, Castle Capital purchased and leased two jets and a helicopter to Penn-Dixie which the parent could have purchased itself for "substantially less than its leasing costs."

Why was Castle taking assets out of one pocket and putting them into the other? The special counsel wasn't sure, but said there was "some evidence that Mr. Castle intended, in large measure by effecting lease transactions with Penn-Dixie, to increase the value of Castle Capital . . . as part of a larger plan in which he would assume his personal control of Castle Capital (which had acquired a large block of Penn-Dixie stock) and thereby increase his personal control of Penn-Dixie."

Meanwhile, the investigation found that Castle was also diddling away some of Castle Capital's assets. Following are several examples.

In December 1972, Castle Capital invested $200,000 in a Long Island real estate venture and later sold ninety percent of its interest to Mr. Castle and eight of his associates. Each was to pay $24,000 to Castle Capital, but few made all the payments, and Mr. Castle saw that no pressure was exerted to collect the money. The real estate venture went down the tubes in November 1975 and the investments were worthless. Castle Capital repaid the investors, including Mr. Castle, for whatever they had put in, and the leasing company wrote the whole thing off.

In 1975, Mr. Castle took it upon himself to put Castle Capital into the race horse business. Since corporate ownership of race horses is not permitted in New York State, Castle put the horses in his name, but the money came from the corporation. As a result of this venture, which the report said was "undertaken primarily to enable Mr. Castle to portray himself to the world as a sportsman," the corporation wound up at least $110,000 poorer.

The race horse business was responsible for another financial bath. Castle Capital made a number of loans to a race horse company and in 1976 had to write off $225,000 to cover the expected loss on the loans.

Listed by the special counsel among an assortment of other alleged malfeasances is this brassy coup: In 1975, Penn-Dixie paid Mr. Castle $6,000 for his interest in the Castle Recycling Corporation. The deal was made within days after regulatory authorities had held that Castle Recycling would have to be shut down for failure to comply with environmental laws.

With the end of the Castle era, Penn-Dixie is struggling to right itself. The board has been completely reconstituted, and is heavily weighted with outside directors. Among the first actions of the board's audit committee was to get rid of the horses, the jet, and the apartments in Miami and Chicago. The Hampshire House apartment was also put on the market. As to the millions allegedly siphoned out of the company, the firm's attorney said that Penn-Dixie has instituted "substantial litigation" to recoup.

CHAPTER THIRTEEN

Victor Posner

King of the Perks

VICTOR POSNER is described by a business consultant as an extremely energetic man with a quick mind who knows more about his companies than one might expect. "He has a knack for picking good operating people so he can concentrate on policy. He works hard, for long hours, and is probably one of the best entrepreneurs in the United States, a risk-oriented person who wins more often than he loses."

But, as can be gleaned from an exhaustive report prepared under an SEC judgment, Posner too has difficulty separating, in his own mind, corporate money from personal money. This confusion led to a long proceeding which ended up with repayment to his various corporations of $1.7 million. This represented money used to support a lifestyle, for Posner and his family, that would probably have been the envy of an oil sheik.

There were yachts, speedboats, jet planes, a riding stable, domestic help, limousines, Jaguars, a Mercedes, a Stutz,

131

penthouse apartments at the Plaza Hotels in New York and Miami, and summer places in Westhampton. There were vacation trips to well-known resorts, liquor bills, restaurant bills, grocery bills, and even five-figure, personal telephone bills—all paid for by one or more of the Posner companies.

The sixty-year-old Posner is chief executive officer and controlling stockholder of a mind-boggling conglomeration of public corporations, subsidiaries, affiliates, and real estate ventures. Of the public corporations, the largest operating company is Sharon Steel, which in 1977 earned about $20 million, after taxes, on a volume of just over $400 million. In 1978 Sharon earned close to $37 million.

In 1969, Posner wrested control of Sharon Steel from a recalcitrant management in a bitterly fought contest. Using NVF Company, a vulcanized fiber producer which he had taken over three years earlier, as the vehicle for the acquisition, Posner came out a winner. The feat was all the more remarkable since NVF paid no cash. Instead the company issued about $100 million in subordinated debentures, and some warrants, in exchange for 1,415,235 shares of Sharon Steel stock. This gave NVF an eighty-six percent interest in Sharon, or complete control. It was a classic example of a small, aggressive company taking over a large, conservative one through the use of what the investment community called Chinese money.

The SEC began a formal investigation into the affairs of the Posner companies on July 20, 1976, looking into the accuracy of financial reports issued by the companies, and into the question of personal benefits to some of the officers and directors of the corporation.

The investigation revealed a pervasive pattern of corporate payments for the personal pleasures of Posner, his thirty-five-year-old son, Steven, and his daughter Gail Posner Cohen. There were also some relatively minor personal expenditures for a brother, Bernard, and other company officials.

In September of 1977, the SEC filed a formal complaint in

federal court in Washington, D.C., outlining its charges, and simultaneously filed a consent judgment. As is the case in most SEC settlements, the defendants didn't admit that they did anything wrong, but agreed not to do it again. The judgment directed that Victor, Steven, and Gail repay the companies a total of $600,000 (which they agreed to do) and noted that this payment would not preclude the companies from making further claims against the Posners for non-business payments.

On top of the usual boilerplate enjoining the Posners and the companies, their "officers, agents, servants, affiliates, successors, subsidiaries, assignees and employees" from violating securities laws, the judgment decreed a further investigation and a report with findings and recommendations. The ground rules which were laid out in the decree directed that an audit committee, composed of two independent directors and one other director, be set up by each company and that these committees oversee the investigation and prepare a report. James J. Needham, a former chairman of the New York Stock Exchange and an expert in the field of corporate governance, served as chairman of the Sharon Steel and the NVF audit committees, and of a twelve-member joint audit committee representing all the Posner companies involved in the proceeding.

The report was completed and filed on November 22, 1978, and the text ran for 211 fun-filled pages. It was supplemented with a series of appendices going from A to G (appendix E was an eleven-page log of all personal flights on corporate aircraft from 1969 to 1977).

The essence of the report: the Posners should pay another $1.1 million back to the corporations, and a major overhaul of corporate controls was required. After some negotiation, the Posners agreed to repay the entire amount, and better controls were installed.

Carrying the formidable title, "Report of the Audit Committee of Sharon Steel Corporation, NVF Company, DWG

Corporation, Pennsylvania Engineering Corporation, South-eastern Public Service Company, (and) Wilson Brothers Pursuant to the Final Judgment in *SEC* v *Sharon Steel Corporation et al.,* Civil Action No. 77-1631," the document spelled out the details of corporate-style luxury living.

Before going ahead with the fun part, let's get some of the structural information out of the way and place the activities in proper perspective: The corporations involved are all controlled by Victor Posner and his family, through ownership of a relatively small percentage of the stock in each. The majority of the shares are in the hands of the public, and since the SEC is responsible for protecting public stockholders, the agency must concern itself with how stockholders' money is spent.

At the apex of the industrial complex sits Victor Posner and Security Management Corporation, a wholly-owned, Posner family, holding company. Security Management holds some stock in the public corporations, plus 83.14 percent of Universal Housing and Development Company, a real estate developer.

The public companies fall into three groups: NVF and its eighty-six percent owned subsidiary, Sharon Steel; DWG Corporation and its subsidiaries, Southeastern Public Service Company and Wilson Brothers; and Pennsylvania Engineering Corporation, which also has a number of subsidiaries and divisions.

Security Management, the Posner holding company, owns 15.3 percent of NVF; and Victor Posner owns 3.5 percent. Convertible securities outstanding could increase the Posner holdings to 40.6 percent.

NVF, in addition to its eighty-six percent interest in Sharon Steel, manufactures vulcanized fibre, industrial laminated plastics, specialty papers, and containers. It also has fifty-one percent interest in Steel Corporation of Texas, a steel service center which warehouses and sells steel products. Some of these come from Sharon, a steel producer. Sharon also mines metallurgical coal and manufactures stainless steel pipe, tubing, and steel strapping. NVF earned $19,965,000 on sales of $502,889,000 in 1977, most of which were attributable to its interest in Sharon Steel.

DWG is essentially a holding company, 17.7 percent owned by Posner interests. The Posner stake could be increased to 54.1 percent based on convertible securities outstanding.

DWG owns National Propane Corporation, a distributor of liquified petroleum gas. It also has a fifty-one percent interest in Southeastern Public Service, which services utilities and municipalities, sells propane gas, produces natural gas and oil, and conducts a refrigeration operation.

Another partially owned DWG subsidiary is Wilson Brothers, a manufacturer and importer of men's and boy's apparel. DWG owns 42.4 percent of Wilson Brothers, and Security Management holds 4.9 percent. DWG reported after tax profits of $4,628,000 on sales of $152,758,000 in 1977.

The Pennsylvania Engineering group is 13.8 percent owned by Security Management and 2.1 percent by Victor Posner. Conversion of outstanding securities could increase Posner interests to about 30 percent. The company does engineering and design and construction of heavy capital equipment, principally for the steel industry. Its 91-percent-owned subsidiary, Birdsboro Corporation, produces steel mill machinery and related equipment. Pennsylvania Engineering netted $3,006,000 on sales of $95,504,000 in 1977.

With this kind of an industrial base, it is not surprising that the Posner family could live well. The unpleasantness arose over the question of whose money they were living on.

Let's start with company-owned yachts. Sharon bought its first yacht in 1969, the year NVF took control of the steel company. It was a modest craft, purchased for $190,000. The purchase was duly approved by Sharon's board, and over the next three years the company absorbed expenses totaling $242,834 related to the yacht, *Sharon S.* The boat was used for some company business but the audit committee could find no logs or other records.

The company disposed of the *Sharon S* in 1971, and after

three yachtless years, stepped up in class by buying, in November 1974, a 102-foot number for $600,000 from a business associate of Victor Posner. The new yacht, originally called *Miss Lauderhill*, was renamed *Sharon S II*, and a dock was built behind Posner's house at Sunset Island in Miami Beach to base her.

Keeping the craft at Posner's house saved the company about $10,000 a year in docking charges, but there were other costs. The company paid $9,460 to build the docking facilities and $107,000 to repair damages to the *Sharon S II*, and an even larger yacht purchased later, because the water behind Posner's house was too shallow. Both ran aground and suffered heavy hull damage.

In the spring of 1976, the *Sharon S II* was repurchased by the seller, and Posner made another move upward. On April 16, 1976, the *Sharon S II* was replaced by *Claybeth*, a $1.5 million job. The purchase was authorized by the executive committee of the Sharon board before the purchase and ratified by the full board afterwards. It was renamed *Sharon S* and housed at the Sunset Island house until March 1977, when it was moved to the Jockey Club, where it remained.

The committees found that, between 1974 and 1976, Victor Posner often used the yachts for outings with friends and family; and Gail Posner Cohen, when staying at the Sunset Island house, frequently took her children or other companions aboard and charged the expenses to the companies. Company expenses related to the two large yachts, from 1974 through 1977, not counting the purchase price, came to $1,079,030.

There were logs and registers covering the use of the yachts, but they were incomplete. Based on an analysis of the logs and other evidence, the committees concluded that at least forty percent of the use was personal and a maximum of twenty-five to thirty percent could be identified as business use. The report noted that personal use dropped sharply once the yacht was moored at the Jockey Club rather than at Sunset Island.

Aside from the use of the yachts, there were other fringe benefits from having the boats at Victor Posner's house. The captain was responsible for all the food and liquor consumed on board. He had a company credit card and access to restaurants where Sharon Steel had had charge accounts. "Many of the items he purchased were for the benefit of Mr. Posner and his family or friends," the audit committee concluded.

Food and liquor consumed in the Sunset Island house by Posner, his family and friends, were paid for with the yacht captain's expense account, as were maintenance expenses for the house and grounds, gifts, and other items. Ultimately, these bills were paid by Sharon Steel. The audit committee's report stated the following:

> During the periods when Victor Posner lived at the Victorian Plaza Hotel (in nearby Bal Harbour, Fla.), he and a personal guest often went to the house and ate dinner either on the boat or in the house. These meals, whether consumed on the boat or in Victor Posner's house, were cooked on the boat by the yacht cook. When Mr. Posner and his guests, or Ms. Cohen and her family or friends, decided to eat in the house, the food was cooked on the boat and then brought up to the house and served by members of the yacht crew.

The yacht captain served as gofer when Victor and Gail ordered restaurant meals brought to the house. He either picked up the food or had it delivered, and the costs were charged to Sharon Steel as yacht expenses. Furthermore, the yacht captain regularly paid to have Victor Posner's house cleaned, and paid the maintenance expenses for the lawn and grounds around the house and for the swimming pool.

Why were these expenses approved by Sharon's top financial officers? The Sunset Island house was considered an extension of the yacht, and the yacht and house a single entertainment facility.

Finally, when the yachts were taken on trips, the captain was expected to pay for purchases on shore, including personal items for guests of Victor Posner who were on the boat.

The audit committee decided that it would give Posner the benefit of the doubt and not recommend that he pay back the costs of buying and maintaining the yachts, but that he should be made to reimburse the company for forty percent of the operating costs. This was calculated at $134,971. After crediting Posner with $25,000 out of the $600,000 settlement, the net amount due the company was put at $109,971.

While yachts can be fun, the real action on water comes with speedboats. Starting in 1969, with a Higgins Magnum purchased by DWG for $11,668, the Posner companies owned a succession of three speedboats, each was a high-performance racing craft, and each was more expensive than its predecessor. There was no evidence of business use for any of them.

The first speedboat, kept at various times at the Fontainebleau Hotel in Miami Beach or at the Sunset Island house, was sold for $2,379 in April 1978. Number two was a 1973 model Cigarette which DWG bought for $20,035. In March 1974, it was sold off for $3,260. The latest was a 1974 model Cigarette bought for $24,993. It was kept at the Sunset house initially and, in the summer of 1976, was shipped to Westhampton where Steven rented a summer house (also on the company). It was returned to Miami in the spring of 1977, repaired, and then sent to the Jockey Club where it remained. According to the audit committee, there was no business justification for any of the speedboats, and the committee recommended that the companies seek a return of $93,836 to cover the cost of the boats and their operating expenses.

During the same year that Sharon Steel was buying its first yacht and DWG its speedboat (1969), Sharon's executive committee authorized the purchase of a Lockheed Jetstar. The basic plane cost $1,750,000 and there was another $400,000 tacked on for a custom interior and extra electronic equipment. The plane was to be delivered April 1, 1970, and in the meantime a used Jetstar was leased for six months at a cost of $100,000. The Jetstar was to be used to transport Sharon executives to areas difficult to reach by commercial craft, to bring customers to Sharon's plants, and to entertain important customers. It was also suggested that NVF, Pennsylvania Engineering, and DWG might use the aircraft on a fee basis.

Four years later Victor Posner decided that a second, larger plane was needed to carry more passengers, provide more privacy, and to impress prominent business guests. Sharon's board authorized the purchase of a British jet, a BAC-111, for $2,100,000.

While the audit committee's report conceded that the planes were used principally for business, it found that many flights were clearly personal. The appendix lists eighty-nine flights over the nine-year period classified as personal. Destinations included such popular vacation spots as Jamaica, Miami, Vero Beach, Atlantic City, Nassau, Grand Island, Monticello, and San Juan. Using a complicated formula based on the operating costs of the aircraft and the number of hours of personal use, the audit committee concluded that Victor Posner should be charged $114,878; Gail Posner $124,435; and Walter Gregg, Sharon's chief financial officer, $7,017. After crediting Victor and Gail with a portion of the SEC settlement, the report concluded that Victor still owed $63,678 and Gail $49,435. The Gregg charge remained at $7,017. In toto, the committee figured that $120,130 was due the company for personal use of the aircraft.

The next issue taken up by the audit committee was the matter of chauffeurs and limousines. The companies maintained two chauffeured limousines for Victor Posner, one in New York and another in Miami Beach. The limousines were used for business and personal purposes, but no logs were kept. Nevertheless, the audit committee concluded that these limousines were additional remuneration "incident to their offices" and let it go at that.

But the chauffeured limousine provided for Gail Posner Cohen, whose services for the companies were rather obscure, was found to be ninety percent personal. The salaries and expenses of the chauffeurs were paid by DWG and came to $127,845. Based on the ninety-percent estimate, the audit committee found she owed $115,060. Crediting her for $70,000 paid in the settlement, the report said the companies should go after another $45,060.

Besides the limos, the companies maintained a fleet of other cars for senior officers. Prior to December 1977, when the companies adopted a standard policy on automobiles, some officers were provided with two or even three automobiles regardless of whether there was a business need for them. The cars were regarded as additional compensation.

Steven Posner was given a Stutz, and a personal friend of Victor Posner was given a Mercedes Benz. From 1975 until March 1978, when the Posner family holding company took over the lease payments on Steven's Stutz, DWG paid out $6,704 on the auto. The committee found that, since Steven already had a company limo and chauffeur, the Stutz was strictly personal and told the company to get its $6,704 back (Steven agreed to pay it). As to the Mercedes, the cost to the company for lease payments and repairs totaled $28,711, or $18,711 more than provided in the SEC settlement. The companies should go after that difference, the committee said.

Among the miscellaneous cars maintained by the company and sometimes used personally by the Posners and friends were two Jaguars kept as pool cars, a Corvette rented for Steven Posner, and a Ford Thunderbird given each year by the Ford Motor Company to an auto leasing subsidiary, apparently in appreciation for the leasing company's business. Because of the difficulties in determining the extent and cost of personal use of these cars, the committee decided to let this item ride. It made no recommendations for reimbursement.

Next came the penthouse at the Plaza. In February 1974, the

Posner companies moved from a fifth floor suite at the Plaza
to a larger, combination, office/residence penthouse at an
annual rental of $100,000. The apartment served as New York
offices for the companies and living quarters for Victor Posner
when in New York. It had a reception area, offices, a kitchen
and dining facility, conference rooms, recreation rooms, and
residential space. The residential portion included four bed-
rooms, a wine vault, a living room, card parlor, and a game
room. It was reserved for Victor Posner and guests. The
companies gave up the Plaza suite in October 1976, having
rented a $100,000-a-year suite at the Waldorf for Posner in
June of that year.

In justifying his expenses at the Plaza and the Waldorf,
Victor Posner contended that as a resident of Miami, he was
entitled to have his living expenses paid by the companies
when in New York on company business. He made frequent
trips to New York, entertained business associates, and worked
long hours. The Waldorf suite was also available for other
company executives.

The audit committees decided that both suites had served a
"substantial business purpose" and the companies should
make no claim for reimbursement. There were some personal
charges at the Plaza drug store, beauty parlor, room service
and meal charges, that were not justified. The committees
figured these at $4,039 for Victor and $15,454 for Gail. Personal charges at the Waldorf came to a piddling $740.

Another Plaza apartment was rented for son Steven when he
was transferred to New York from Miami. The apartment was
supposed to be "temporary," until he could find a permanent
residence. Steven moved into the seven-room suite with his
wife, three children, and domestic help at the end of 1974. He
stayed for nearly two years. During that period the companies
paid the rent, room service, laundry, dry cleaning, food,
entertainment, and all living expenses. Living expenses added
up to $106,384, and the rent came to $178,371—for a monthly
cost of about $16,400.

Steven Posner's mission in New York was to become more

deeply involved in financial matters and to develop and strengthen relationships with bankers and other members of the New York financial community.

He made some effort to get an apartment but had difficulty finding something he regarded as suitable. The audit committee found that the problem was caused by his strict standards. For a long time he didn't even consider rental apartments because he wanted the tax advantages of a cooperative. He wanted a minimum of 8,000 to 10,000 square feet of space, only upper floors, and was particular about the location and cost.

To determine what would be a reasonable time to allow Steven to live on the companies before getting his own place, Price Waterhouse was engaged to survey eleven companies comparable to the Posner group and find out for how long they would make these kinds of relocation payments. Of the eleven, none said they would pay for more than sixty days. The committees concluded that since the board expected the companies to pick up Steven's expenses for a period of time, and since he did try to find his own place, and was, after all, a high-ranking officer, he was entitled to one hundred twenty days of living on the companies.

Summers in New York can be beastly, even in a seven-room suite at the Plaza; so Steven rented a house in Westhampton, Long Island, in the summer of 1975 and another Westhampton place in the summer of 1976. By now you can guess who paid the rent. That's right, the Posner companies. (The second house was leased through 1978, and though the companies paid the 1976 and 1977 rent, they did not pay in 1978.) After a little corporate hocus pocus, the house appeared on a resolution presented to the board of directors. The resolution declared that the house should "be deemed to be for an ordinary and necessary business purpose." The resolution came on December 2, 1977, about two months after the SEC judgment was entered, but before the audit committees were appointed.

The committees took the position that the resolution was not retroactive and pursued the investigation. According to their report, Steven said he took the Westhampton houses, to improve the companies' relationships with the financial and investment community. He said that many of the investment and banking people with whom he made contact when he first arrived in New York spent weekends during the summer in Westhampton. Mr. Posner said that there was an opportunity to enhance his relationships with these people by going with them to Westhampton, and to meet with them socially, but with an ultimate business purpose of improving the companies' financial and investment relationships."

The cost for rent in Westhampton for three years (1975, 1976, and 1977) was $95,378, with additional expenses totaling $39,991—for a grand total of $135,369. Steven provided some records with dates and names of weekend guests. Based on these incomplete records, the committees decided "that it would not be inappropriate or unfair to Mr. Posner to assume that he incurred as much as $10,000 worth of expenses per summer in entertaining business guests, and that any additional expenses were personal." With this formula, the committees concluded that Steven owed the companies $108,773 for personal expenses.

In addition to the Plaza and the Waldorf in New York, the audit committees looked into the rental of space and company-financed renovations at the Victorian Plaza Hotel, Miami Beach, Florida, both from the point of view of personal use and for possible conflicts of interest. The Victorian Plaza is owned by a trust created by Victor Posner for the benefit of himself and his family. A number of its apartments were set aside for executives and business guests, and in 1973 the Posner companies moved their headquarters into the building.

Victor Posner, himself, used seven apartments in the Victorian Plaza. One suite had a pool table, a lounging area, and a large television set. Another had a bar and dining area, and a desk and working area. Two were his personal quarters, and two others were bedroom apartments used as guest rooms. The seventh was an office.

The corporate headquarters move followed a search of the Miami area by a committee of company executives (including Steven Posner). The committee said that it had trouble finding a building with sufficient parking space and which provided elevator and air-conditioning services after 5 P.M. or on weekends. It recommended taking space in Mr. Posner's building where ample parking and round-the-clock services were available.

The original SEC complaint made some substantial charges relating to the use of the Victorian Plaza. The SEC contended that Posner-controlled companies paid higher rents at the Victorian Plaza than non-affiliated tenants, and higher than the market for comparable space in the area. The SEC figured this overcharge at $100,000. Also, the SEC said maid service charges for rooms occupied by Posner-controlled companies "were at least twice the fair market value of such services." The SEC further charged that DWG spent a "substantial amount of money" to renovate the Victorian Plaza lobby and that $1 million was spent by Posner companies to renovate the sixteenth and seventeenth floors where Victor Posner had his seven apartments. It was the SEC contention that Victor Posner personally benefitted from the $44,000-a-year Victorian Plaza suite.

In settling the SEC case, $68,600 was judged to have been spent for Victor Posner's personal use of rooms and another $75,000 for decorating and refurbishing. The audit committees found that rental charges to Posner-controlled companies were not out of line, and that maid service charges were fair. They found that rents charged for residential apartments occupied by Posner-controlled companies in some cases were identical with others in the building, sometimes higher, and sometimes lower. From May 1973 to September 1977, the committees estimated a net overcharge of $17,429, which the companies should try to get back.

The committees estimated Victor's personal benefit from rooms at the Victorian Plaza at $93,770, or $25,170 more than he paid in settling with the SEC. On the remodeling, the committees said costs of $161,780 relate directly to Victor Posner's personal living quarters and that he should pay the companies another $86,780 on top of the $75,000 already paid.

In renovating the lobby of the Victorian Plaza, the Posner-controlled companies spent about $40,000. Finding that it was the responsibility of the landlord, the committees recommended that Victor Posner repay $25,000 in addition to the $15,000 paid earlier.

The committees also looked into the use of a group of houses, a meeting complex, and a barn in the area around Yorklyn, Delaware, where NVF made its headquarters. It found that the houses and meeting rooms were essentially used for business purposes (the houses served for business guests). No business use could be found for the barn, which was unused and in disrepair until 1975 when Victor Posner suggested that the firm buy some horses. The horses would be an added attraction for business guests, Posner said at the time.

The barn was repaired and horses acquired, but the evidence showed that "there were only a handful of occasions during this period (1975, 1976, 1977) when someone, who could be fairly categorized as a business relation, rode the horses." Instead, most of the riding was done by Victor Posner and his family for their own personal pleasure.

The committees came up with a formula for apportioning the costs of maintaining the riding operation and concluded that Victor Posner should pay the company $25,121 out of the $65,021 it cost to maintain the horses during the three-year period.

There were a number of apartments in the Victorian Plaza Hotel provided for various officers, and in most cases the committees felt they were business related or could be classified as additional compensation; so the companies had no claim. However, in the case of Bernard Posner, Victor's brother, the report recommended some reimbursement. First, there was some $17,661 in rent that Sharon Steel paid for Bernard's apartment at the Victorian Plaza, which the committee said "transferred the burden" of paying for his Miami Beach residence from him to Sharon Steel (Bernard had maintained his own apartment in the area before he moved into the Victorian Plaza). The report also found that the companies paid out $26,285 in rent for an apartment, on New York's fashionable East Side, that was really Bernard's primary residence. Finally, it was recommended that the companies seek $5,748, paid out for Bernard's Pittsburgh apartment during the one year that it was his primary residence.

It was Gail Posner Cohen who, the committees found, rang up prodigious phone bills which the companies paid. Gail was a director of all the companies, and held titles as an officer of some of them, but did not participate in management nor receive any salaries. She did receive some director's fees. The committees noted that she had resigned all her titles as of April 20, 1978 and did not plan to stand for reelection to the boards of any of the companies.

Ms. Cohen gave the committees little cooperation. She did not show up for examination and refused to disclose an unlisted number from which she made calls, charged to the companies.

Between May 1, 1974 and March 31, 1977, the companies paid out $13,480 for Ms. Cohen's telephone bills. The audit committees reported:

> The companies were not able to furnish the audit committees with the precise costs incurred by them for these telephones between January 1970 and April 1974. The telephone bills covering this period show only the telephone numbers and do not indicate the addresses of the telephones included in the bill, and Ms. Cohen maintained an unlisted number during the period between January 1970 and April 1974. The audit committees were unable to obtain Ms. Cohen's unlisted number and

requested the number from her counsel, who subsequently advised the audit committees that he was unsuccessful in his efforts to obtain Ms. Cohen's number.

Unable to get precise information, the committees averaged out Ms. Cohen's monthly telephone costs during the period for which information was available, applied this average to the fifty-two months during which there were no figures, and came up with $20,020 due for the use of the unlisted phone.

In 1978, Ms. Cohen lived at Victor Posner's Sunset Island House, where phone bills were paid by the companies. Victor Posner has not lived in that house since January, but the phone bills nevertheless mounted up to $5,582, which the committees said Gail should repay and which she has agreed to do.

In addition to investigating personal expenditures and recommending recovery, the committees included a long section of suggestions for tightening up controls. Among the recommendations were establishment of a "common costs center" to equitably allocate costs among the companies, reduction of the size of the various boards of directors, and reorganization of the boards so that independent directors would be in the majority.

The committees also recommended a review of the uses of corporate assets to determine if they constitute ordinary and necessary business expenses and if they produce a reasonable benefit to the corporation. The review should be conducted at least once a year, and the audit committees should report their findings to the respective board. And for starters, the committee said, boards should promptly review the need for retaining the following: the yacht, speed boats, airplanes, special life insurance for individuals, company apartments, and offices and apartments at the Victorian Plaza.

The committees said that the companies should—

• try to reduce the high cost of company aircraft by more

frequent business use or through spot leasing, charter, or commercial flights;
- review the special insurance policies with the view toward selling them to the beneficiaries or cashing them in;
- provide company apartments only with the specific approval of the respective board of directors;
- consider moving out of the Victorian Plaza "to avoid all appearance of conflict of principles."

As a result of the SEC investigation and the final judgment, the Posners agreed to repay $600,000. The subsequent investigation by the audit committees resulted in another $1.1 million being returned to the company.

But investigations of this sort don't come cheap. Ignoring the cost to taxpayers of the SEC's work, the follow-up probe involved four separate audit committees, an assortment of prestigious law firms (the report itself was written by Arnold and Porter of Washington, D.C.), a total of fifteen separate studies by two major accounting firms (Price Waterhouse and Company, and Arthur Andersen and Company) and untold man-hours put in by the staff of the Posner companies in searching out and providing information.

As we all know, prestigious lawyers and Big-Eight accounting firms are as expensive as yachts and penthouse apartments, if not nearly as much fun. A source close to the investigation estimated that the total cost of the work that went into producing the audit committees' report exceeded $2 million. The net effect to stockholders of the Posner companies was that it cost about two dollars for every one dollar collected. Hardly what can be classified as a cost-effective exercise.

It is hoped, however, that there will be future benefits to public stockholders through better controls based on the recommendations in the report, and the entire affair might incline Posner himself to think twice before buying another yacht. The change in the tax law in 1978 might also inhibit him somewhat. There is also the hope that all public stockholders will benefit from whatever deterrent effect the case may have on the perk-abusing proclivities of corporate management in general.

In fairness to Victor Posner, I think it should be pointed out that the committees were favorably impressed with the bottom line results of his management, another factor which clearly separates Mr. Posner from Mr. Castle. Said the audit committees, "Since Victor Posner acquired control of the companies, they have generally achieved profitability and substantial growth in sales. The audit committees believe that the business success of the companies represents a significant accomplishment by Mr. Posner and the other officers of the companies responsible for management during this period."

Thus, one might wonder if stockholders might not have been better off letting Mr. Posner indulge himself a bit, so long as there was still plenty of cash left over for the rest of them.

CHAPTER FOURTEEN

The Outlook

Fair and Milder

CORPORATE MANAGEMENT has been less than thrilled about the SEC's pressing for disclosure to stockholders of all those little perquisite goodies: disclosure provides new ammunition for corporate gadflies who harass management at annual meetings. Even more disturbing is the prospect of stepped up activity by the IRS on the coattails of the SEC initiative. Some feel that the cost of keeping track of the perks may exceed the cost of the perks themselves. One executive, quoted in *Business Week,* saw the SEC program as possibly creating "an immense bookkeeping effort to uncover a gnat for all the world's stockholders to see."

Joseph E. Elmlinger, a partner in the accounting firm of Deloitte Haskins and Sells, told me in an interview, that although the SEC program will spur management to take a closer look at perks and perhaps move more toward direct cash remuneration to executives, perks are not going to be eliminated. "We're still going to have them, but they will be monitored more closely. I don't think we'll see a flood of sales of corporate airplanes."

On the question of disclosure, Elmlinger said there should be "some kind of balance between disclosure and the meaningful conduct of business." He added that the problem is to decide on a "threshold" amount so that corporations would not be required to disclose "every last dollar." Too much disclosure can be misleading, Elmlinger said. "The public might get the impression that a business corporation is being run solely for the benefit of management. This is not the case. Furthermore, increasing the amount of disclosure in a financial situation will not necessarily lead to a better-informed public. If you clutter up disclosures, you end up not disclosing anything. More does not necessarily mean better. People are turned off by all the boilerplate. You know, corporate disclosures are not written in the style of a popular novel."

Edwin S. Mruk, a director of the accounting firm of Arthur Young and Company, and an expert in executive recruitment and the design of executive compensation packages, said he thought the SEC disclosure requirement will cause some companies to rethink their perk program and maybe there will be some retrenchment. "This is not because there is anything wrong with perks but because corporate management is reluctant to make waves."

In structuring compensation plans for executives, Mruk said that perks have to make sense for both the company and the executive:

> I think it is important that the executive have a say in what he believes he needs. Recently we were working with the vice-president for international operations of a client. He was required to do a lot of traveling and asked that the company compensate him for the cost of bringing his wife along on at least two trips a year. I thought this was a legitimate request, and although it would have to be considered remuneration to the executive, he would still come out ahead. In the fifty percent bracket, he'd have to earn $20,000 to pay for a $10,000 trip. If

the company pays for it, he'll have income of $10,000 and have to pay a tax of $5,000. Besides, the perk made sense for him. If an executive on the domestic side wanted the same perk, just because someone else is getting it, his chances would not be particularly good.

In making the point that perks must be reasonable in individual situations, another compensation expert, vice-president of an international drug company, told of one his company refused to grant. It seems a certain executive was under doctors' instructions to swim four laps a day in his pool because of a heart condition. "He told us we would have to be prepared to put a bubble on his pool and to heat it so he could use it the year round. We didn't hire him."

Perks are subject to changes with the times and conditions. Provisions for personal security, such as chauffeur-body guards, are among the fastest growing perks. This is particularly true in overseas areas such as Italy, where the kidnapping of executives has become a national pastime.

"I know if I went to Italy on business, I'd expect more than cab fare," said Arthur Young's Mruk. He added that there is also a trend away from the chauffeured limousines to non-attention-getting station wagons. "A chauffeured car is a natural target. Why make it so obvious?" he said.

Although this country has not had the kind of terrorism that has swept across much of Europe, companies here are aware of the danger and are taking no chances with their key executives. There are now schools for executives and their drivers in which they are given instructions on how to avoid ambush. One tactic: the "bootleg" turn, in which the driver jams on the emergency brake, swings the steering wheel, and in an instant the car is turned 180 degrees and speeding in the opposite direction—just like on television.

Because of the heat emanating from the SEC and the IRS on the traditional perks, compensation specialists are busy seeking out new and innocuous-looking fringe benefits. One suggestion from Arthur Young is a corporate education loan program. The corporation lends money to the executive to be used for the education of his children. The loans would be repayable over an extended period, perhaps seven or eight years, and would carry a "reasonable" interest charge.

It is doubtful, says the accounting firm, that the perk would be attacked by any of the agencies or the public because of the "very high value placed on education in this country" and because the executive is really paying his own way. From the corporation's point of view, the plan could serve as "golden handcuffs" by providing that the loan be immediately repayable if the executive left the company.

In addition to company planes, country club memberships, and company-owned luxury housing, there are many subtle little privileges that go with corporate rank. The size of the office an executive works in, its location, whether it's carpeted or not, the paintings on the wall, the number of windows, all go under the classification of perks. Some corporations, particularly the large bureaucratic ones, have a highly structured system for determining the number of square feet and type of office for each grade of executive. Generally, it's tied to compensation levels. The more money an executive earns, the larger the office, the better the location, and the more elaborate the furnishings.

Executive dining facilities are also sharply stratified in the corporate world. There are small, private dining rooms for the top officers, equipped with the finest china and sterling silver flatware, where food is served by a staff trained to materialize silently at the precise moment your butter runs out or your water glass is down a half inch. The next level of executive might have to use a dining room with two or three tables in it and several conversations going on at the same time. For the rest of the staff, there's the company cafeteria.

The large banks are the most rigidly structured in providing dining facilities for their executives. Typically, the chairman and president each will have a dining room set aside for exclusive use. Occasionally, the room might be made available for another senior officer if the boss is not going to use it. The next level of executives will have the use of private dining rooms, but generally they must be reserved in advance on a "need" basis. Going down another notch, there would be another room, comparable to a first class restaurant, where officers below the executive or senior vice-president level would entertain their business guests.

Banks are still a bit stiff about serving alcohol on the premises, and many an elegant lunch must be washed down with ice water (served in the finest crystal). At Manufacturers Hanover, dry or sweet sherry is available before lunch at the bank's headquarters. At Chase Manhattan, liquor is not available at the dining rooms in the Chase Plaza headquarters (until after 4 P.M.), but the bank maintains facilities uptown where booze is served before lunch. It's referred to as a "beverage," and when the first is finished, there is no encouragement for a second. But dry or wet, private or public, all corporate dining has a common denominator: its cost is absorbed by the corporation and the IRS.

Although the most visible perks and expense accounts are in advertising, public relations, publishing, popular music, movies, and television, the staid old banking business is no slouch. Bankers try to project an image of conservatism, solidity, and sobriety, but almost all bankers, from the lowly assistant secretary to the board chairman, are in the entertainment business. They entertain depositors, borrowers, potential depositors or borrowers, other bankers . . . in short, the immediate world. Most major banks have blocks of seats for sporting events for the macho types who enjoy watching hockey players busting each other's heads or seven-footers running around in their underwear. For the more cultured, they provide theater, concert, ballet, or opera tickets. Of course, these events include dinner at a high-priced restaurant, and guests are escorted by a banker or a couple of bankers, all traveling first class on the company and the IRS.

One banker told me that if one of his good customers called at four o'clock on a Friday afternoon and wanted tickets for the hottest show in town for that evening, "I'll get them. We have a special department that handles those kinds of requests and we'll get those tickets if we have to spend a hundred bucks a piece with the scalpers."

Another industry which might not be considered particularly lush ground for expense accounts or perks is retailing. Once you get past the selling floor, some great opportunities for expense account living open up. In retailing you can work both sides of the expense account coin—as entertainor and entertainee.

Retailers buy merchandise from manufacturers, and manufacturers are a notoriously grateful lot. Some have been known to express their gratitude with Cadillacs and color television sets and even with plain brown envelopes stuffed with fancy green bills. But again, this type of illegal conduct is not within the province of this exposition. You don't have to be a crook to enjoy the fruits of the expense account society.

A national survey by *Men's Wear Magazine*, a Fairchild publication, showed that, starting with assistant buyers, expense account money becomes available. Assistant buyers have some travel expenses and allowances for lunches with resources (in retailing, suppliers are called resources, perhaps because suppliers doesn't tell the whole story). The survey did not make clear who was paying for the lunches—the assistant buyer's company or the resource's—but for our purposes, this makes no difference. The assistant buyer obviously wouldn't have to pay.

Moving up to buyers, they all have expense accounts for buying trips. Divisional merchandise managers get T&E money and incentive bonuses for sweeteners. At the top, in retailing, there have been some eye-popping contracts. For example, Angelo Arena went over from Neiman Marcus, the stylish Texas specialty chain, to head Chicago's Marshall Field and Company in 1977 at an annual salary of $300,000 plus stock options. Perks included $500,000 toward purchase of suitable housing, paid education for his five children, and a chauffeured limousine.

As indicated by the many examples mentioned earlier, the large public companies do their best to provide top executives with privileges and facilities to improve their business performance and which may have incidental personal benefits. It has also been amply illustrated that when the executive is in a position to push the board of directors around, the benefits are often considerably more than incidental.

Amenities make the pressures and pains of the corporate jungle more bearable, but the big companies are forever hassled by the SEC or IRS or their own CPAs. This limits freedom of action but leaves plenty of room for good living at corporate expense.

Smaller, privately held companies are less restricted, and if they can't afford a corporate jet, they may be able to provide enough of the other comforts to make it worth your while to put up with commercial flights. The privately held companies don't have to worry about the reaction of public stockholders, and they don't have to file all those reports with the SEC. Of course, even private companies must face up to the tax man and their own accountants, but the smaller ones don't have the same visibility as the giants. The IRS tends to follow the same basic rule as the rest of us: go where the money is. The larger a company, the closer IRS scrutiny it will get.

So a small, profitable company could be the best bet, at least for the more common perks. In my own experience, which has been rather closely tied to the garment industries, the company Cadillac or Mercedes is standard equipment. You get an inside man, an outside man, a designer, an office, and a limo; and you're in business. You can't even go broke in the garment field unless you have a chauffeured limo to drive you down to the courthouse to file bankruptcy papers.

In small concerns, the company car mentality filters down from owners to middle management, and many a production or sales manager has a company car and a gasoline credit card. There is no foolishness about what portion constitutes business use and what can be considered "incidental personal benefits." The company pays for the car and all the gasoline charges, and who is to complain. The SEC is not involved; the IRS is busy elsewhere; and even if it does audit a smaller company, it's virtually impossible to determine what portion is business and what is personal.

Is the whole expense account, perks system unfair? Sure it's unfair. President Carter, in campaigning against expense account excesses, pointed out that the average American doesn't have the benefits of three-martini lunches or a yacht, and, if he has a small boat, it's not tax deductible. The President cited a businessman who charged off 338 "so-called business lunches" in one year, for a total of over $10,000 in deductions, adding that, "the average working American had to pay the guy's taxes for him."

As Swifty Lazar put it, "Carter is a hick." In life, we must deal with reality, fair or foul, and the reality is a continuation (and probably expansion) of the expense account, perks system. From time to time there will be reform movements, such as the SEC's disclosure action, and some extra pressure by the IRS. But federal agencies are no match for the combined forces of economics and human nature. So instead of railing about the unfairness of it all, get in on it. There are billions out there:

Turn in that Brown Paper Bag with the
Egg Salad Mess
For the Green Plastic Card that says
American Express.

Acknowledgments

While this book appears to have been written, it would be more accurate to say it was constructed—brick by brick from a broad range of sources. It is impossible to acknowledge all sources since some provided sensitive material and preferred to remain anonymous. Also, there are ideas that an author draws from his own brain that surely do not spring spontaneously. They are the result of various stimuli that become so muddied in the mind, their origins can no longer be traced.

On the premise that it is better to thank somebody even if you can't thank everybody, I'll make a stab at mentioning some of my more obvious benefactors.

First, I must thank my agent, Artie Pine, who had the faith and fortitude to push the idea of an expense account book from a vague conception to a reality.

Next, in alphabetical order, is a list of those who provided much of the anecdotal material and to whom I am deeply indebted. This list excludes those mentioned by name in the book:

Murray Aboff, Jack Albuquerque, Joan Bergman, Frank Bonura, David Custage, Joseph Duome, Andrew Edson, Bruce Ellig, Edie Fraser, Delayne Gold, Jim Graziano, Heidi Hessenberger, Suzanne Holmes, Mary Alice Kellogg, Becki Levine, Al Levy, Walter Loeb, John Lund, Charles MacMillan, Elliot Meisel, Saul Pankin, Harold Putterman, Susan Raines, Martin Rod, Linda Rosenberg, Patricia Sachs, Bernard Shapiro, Stanley Slom, Dominick Tarantino, Jesse Taub, Dian Terry, Lewis Webel, and Chris Zahariades.

I must also thank the Securities and Exchange Commission for promoting disclosure of the intimate details of the corporate welfare state, and the Internal Revenue Service for providing some helpful information and allowing me to keep enough of my earnings to sustain life and the strength to depress the keys of my typewriter.

Among the publications most liberally drawn upon were the *New York Times,* the *Wall Street Journal,* and *Fortune.* My thanks to these sterling purveyors of business and general intelligence.

Finally, a special thanks to my wife, Adele, for her enthusiasm, criticism, and patience, and most of all, for accepting without question my disclaimer of any first-hand knowledge of expense account sex.

Index